GUIDEBOOK TO

IR

Whiskey

AND OTHER

Distilled Spirits

IN

COLORADO

NEW MEXICO & WYOMING

D0754258

EDITED BY

DOUGLAS M. SACARTO & HOWELL F. WRIGHT

CRAFT
PUBLISHING

ESTES PARK, COLORADO

Cover Photograph Credits
Front Top: Colorado Front Range in Autumn (© Nsirlin | Dreamstime.com)
  Bottom Left: Distillery Thermometer, courtesy of Anvil Distilling (See company profile, p. 60.)
  Bottom Center: Berryoska Cocktail, courtesy of Deviant Spirits (See company profile, p. 68.)
  Bottom Right: Colorado abruzzi rye prior to harvest for the distillery, courtesy of Leopold Bros.
  (See company profile, p. 112.)
Back Cover: Whiskey in the Mountains, courtesy of J'Ann Wright

Please only drink responsibly.

International Standard Book Number: 978-1-7322931-0-6
Library of Congress Control Number: 2018942597

Editors: Douglas M. Sacarto and Howell F. Wright
Design and Production: Douglas M. Sacarto

Published by:
Craft Publishing, LLP
P.O. Box 3213
Estes Park, CO 80517

Printed in the United States of America

ACKNOWLEDGMENTS

THIS *GUIDEBOOK* exists only because of the remarkable concentration of craft spirits and their makers in Colorado and the Mountain West. Their accomplishments are the foundation for the book, and they have contributed the bulk of its contents for us to compile and present as effectively as possible. We celebrate all of them for their industry and the wonderful products they are making, and we offer our deepest appreciation to the owners of the more than sixty companies who supplied photos and detailed information for our two-page profiles of their businesses and their featured products.

Six individuals—five distillers and a professional writer—volunteered, with the merest "would you be interested," to write the initial articles, *pro bono*, that give background and context for the *Guidebook*. We are extremely grateful to David DeFazio, Joe Elkins, Craig Engelhorn, Colin Keegan, Victor Matthews and Lisa Hutchins for their valuable and generous contributions.

We want to thank the following for their time and the expertise they provided in interviews for the article, "Cocktails of the West": Natalie Bovis, Beverage Consultant, The Liquid Muse, Santa Fe, New Mexico; Stephen Gould, Owner, Golden Moon Distillery, Golden, Colorado; Jeremy Hugus, Cocktail Columnist, Casper, Wyoming; Amber Pollack, Owner, Backwards Distilling, Mills, Wyoming; Sujib Timilsina, Bar Manager, Wapiti Bar, Estes Park, Colorado; Ryan White, Owner, Devil's Head Distillery, Englewood, Colorado.

A founder's story also needs to be told about the *Guidebook* and the role of another book and its editor. The idea for the *Guidebook* actually began in Scotland, where Howell Wright and his wife, J'Ann Wright, were touring distilleries. The tour guide was expert about the seventeen sites they visited, but Howell was rather surprised at the extensive details the guide related about many other distilleries they drove past but could not visit. He finally asked the guide, "Duncan, how can you possibly have learned as much as you know about so many distilleries?" Without saying a word, the guide handed Howell a copy of the *Malt Whisky Yearbook* edited by Ingvar Ronde. The *Yearbook* had feature articles and a center section with detailed information about every malt whiskey distillery in Scotland. The idea was born for a similar comprehensive guidebook to promote the local industry here. We happily acknowledge the *Yearbook* and the encouraging advice that Ingvar himself has given.

On a very personal level, we thank our wives, J'Ann Wright and Lisa Hutchins, for their ongoing support and patience, as well as the business and technical contributions they have made to the book and to Craft Publishing.

CONTENTS

LOCATOR
FEATURED BRANDS & PRODUCT TYPES

FEATURED BRANDS	Page	WHISKEY					
		Bourbon	Corn	Malt	Rye	Wheat	Whiskey*
10th Mountain	150	•	•		•		•
3 Hundred Days	132						•
Algodones	184	•	•				•
Anvil	60						•
Axe and the Oak	134	•			•		•
Backwards	192	•		•	•		•
Bear Creek	98	•			•	•	•
Black Bear	136	•	•	•			•
Black Canyon	62	•	•				•
Blue Fish	138	•		•			•
Branch & Barrel	100	•	•				•
Breckenridge Distillery	152	•		•			•
Colorado Gold	140	•	•		•		
Colorado Vodka	102						
CopperMuse	64	•		•			•
Dancing Pines	66	•	•	•	•		•
Deerhammer	168	•	•	•	•		•
Deviant Spirits	68						
Devil's Head	104						
Distillery 291	142	•		•	•		•
Downslope	106			•	•		
Durango Craft Spirits	170	•					•
Elevation 5003	70	•	•	•	•		•
Elkins	72		•				•
Feisty Spirits	74	•	•	•	•	•	•
Geek Spirits	76	•		•	•		
Golden Moon	108	•		•	•		
Honey House	172	•					•
Idlewild Spirits	154	•		•	•		•
Jackson Hole	194	•		•	•		
K J Wood	174	•		•			•
Laws Whiskey	110	•	•	•	•	•	•

* All other whiskey types, Including white/moonshine, flavored and light.

| | OTHER DISTILLED SPIRITS | | | | | |
Agavé	Gin	Liqueur	Rum	Vodka	Region	Page
		•		•	CO-NW	150
					CO-SE	132
	•	•		•	NM	184
	•		•	•	CO-NE	60
		•			CO-SE	134
	•	•	•	•	WY	192
			•	•	METRO	98
			•	•	CO-SE	136
		•		•	CO-NE	62
•			•	•	CO-SE	138
					METRO	100
	•	•	•	•	CO-NW	152
				•	CO-SE	140
				•	METRO	102
	•	•	•	•	CO-NE	64
	•	•	•	•	CO-NE	66
	•				CO-SW	168
	•	•		•	CO-NE	68
	•			•	METRO	104
					CO-SE	142
•	•		•	•	METRO	106
				•	CO-SW	170
	•	•		•	CO-NE	70
					CO-NE	72
		•			CO-NE	74
			•		CO-NE	76
	•	•			METRO	108
			•	•	CO-SW	172
	•	•	•	•	CO-NW	154
	•			•	WY	194
	•			•	CO-SW	174
				•	METRO	110

FEATURED BRANDS & PRODUCT TYPES

FEATURED BRANDS	Page	WHISKEY					
		Bourbon	Corn	Malt	Rye	Wheat	Whiskey*
Left Turn	186	•	•				•
Leopold Bros.	112	•			•		•
Local Distilling	114		•				
Longtucky Spirits	78	•	•	•	•		
Mad Rabbit	116	•	•	•	•		•
Marble Distilling	156	•			•	•	•
Mile High Spirits	118	•					
Mobb Mountain	80			•	•		
Montanya	176						
Mystic Mountain	144	•	•				•
NOCO Distillery	82	•	•	•	•	•	•
Old Elk	84	•					
Old Town	86	•			•		•
Peach Street	158	•			•		•
Rising Sun	120	•			•		•
Rocker Spirits	122	•			•	•	•
Sand Creek	146			•			
Santa Fe Spirits	188			•			
Spirit Hound	88	•		•	•		
Spring44	90				•		•
State 38	124	•		•	•	•	•
Steamboat Whiskey	160	•	•		•	•	•
Still Cellars	92			•	•		•
Stoneyard	162						•
Stranahan's	126			•			
Syntax Spirits	94	•					•
Telluride Distilling	178						•
Whistling Hare	128	•		•	•		•
Wood's High Mountain	180			•	•		
Woody Creek	164	•		•	•		•
Wyoming Whiskey	196	•			•		•
TOTALS		45	19	30	36	8	44

* All other whiskey types, Including white/moonshine, flavored and light.

OTHER DISTILLED SPIRITS						
Agavé	Gin	Liqueur	Rum	Vodka	Region	Page
	•	•	•	•	NM	186
	•	•		•	METRO	112
	•	•			METRO	114
	•	•	•		CO-NE	78
•	•		•	•	METRO	116
	•	•		•	CO-NW	156
	•			•	METRO	118
	•			•	CO-NE	80
			•		CO-SW	176
	•			•	CO-SE	144
•	•		•	•	CO-NE	82
	•			•	CO-NE	84
	•			•	CO-NE	86
•	•	•		•	CO-NW	158
	•	•		•	METRO	120
			•	•	METRO	122
					CO-SE	146
	•	•		•	NM	188
	•	•	•		CO-NE	88
	•	•		•	CO-NE	90
•	•			•	METRO	124
	•			•	CO-NW	160
				•	CO-NE	92
		•			CO-NW	162
					METRO	126
	•		•	•	CO-NE	94
		•		•	CO-SW	178
	•		•	•	METRO	128
	•	•		•	CO-SW	180
	•		•		CO-NW	164
					WY	196
7	38	26	23	45		

WELCOME TO THE *GUIDEBOOK*!

THERE'S A bonanza of liquid treasure expanding across the Mountain West—that is, more than 100 companies making some 200 whiskeys and a total of more than 400 distilled spirits in Colorado, New Mexico and Wyoming. With such a dizzying array of choices, how can you begin to learn about them?

That's where the *Guidebook to Whiskey and Other Distilled Spirits* comes in. It provides a comprehensive list of all active companies and their specialties in the three-state region—organized geographically with in-depth two-page profiles for more than sixty featured brands, describing their production practices and hundreds of craft spirits. In addition, to get you started (whether you're a beginner or expert), we've included seven feature articles that give background and context for the *Guidebook* entries.

Facts about the distilleries, including their business philosophies, distillation and production methods, product descriptions, and tasting notes, were supplied by the companies themselves. Our job is to help tell their stories in the most comprehensive, accessible and easy-to-use way possible. We're not evaluating products or production methods—that'll be up to you—but we do celebrate the richness, innovation and diverse range of craft spirits produced in our tri-state region, full of exciting flavors and world-class quality.

How to use the *Guidebook*

Locator Table—Following the Table of Contents, the four-page Locator lists the sixty-three featured companies alphabetically, as well as the types of distilled spirits they're making. Their geographic region is listed along with the page number of each company's two-page profile. Use this table to identify companies that make the spirit types you're looking for, or as a summary of the distiller's general product line. Note: Some products may still be in the process of aging or otherwise not currently available.

Regional Maps—To plan your distillery and tasting room visits, check the map at the front of each section that shows the location of featured companies in that region.

Two-Page Company Profiles—Each featured brand is listed alphabetically within its region, according to the primary business address (a company may have a separate tasting room in a different region). The profiles tell you about the company's products, business practices, philosophy and production methods, including the company's own tasting notes. Up to four products may be highlighted in each profile, with more detailed information and a bottle photo presented for one of them as their featured product. We've also provided contact and online site info, as well as tasting room and distillery tour availability.

Additional Company Listings—With new distilleries starting each year, some companies are just getting underway, while others were unable to submit their information. But to provide a comprehensive listing, these companies are listed in an appendix, with contact information and product highlights.

Fascinating Reading—We've got seven articles at the beginning of the *Guidebook*, spanning a range of topics that'll whet your thirst:

- ❑ Whiskey devotee, Howell F. Wright, provides an introductory rundown and framework in "Whiskey & Other Distilled Spirits in the Mountain West."
- ❑ Lisa Hutchins explores the new golden age of cocktails now upon us in "Cocktails: A Marvelous Mingling."
- ❑ Three owners, one in each state, describe the challenges, triumphs and lessons learned while building their successful distilleries:
  - Craig Engelhorn—"Have the Right Stuff? Starting Spirit Hound"
  - Colin Keegan—"Under the Apple Tree: How It Happened at Santa Fe Spirits"
  - David F. DeFazio—"The Making of a Wyoming Distillery"
- ❑ Joe T. Elkins of Elkins Distillery examines the critical process of whiskey aging in "Maturing Whiskey in the West: Tradition & Innovation in Craft Distilling"
- ❑ Master Chef and distiller Victor Matthews shares professional techniques and delicious recipes for successful pairings of food and whiskey (or other distilled spirits) in "Matches Made in Heaven: Whiskey & Food Adventures"

Glossary and Index—Located at the end of the *Guidebook*, the glossary helps with definitions for special terms, while the index lets you know where to find specific items you're interested in, such as a certain botanical ingredient or method of production.

Starting Out

With some 400 products to explore, your adventure begins with certain priorities. Products and companies located nearby, with tasting rooms where you can sample spirits before buying a full bottle, certainly will be primary destinations.

The *Guidebook*'s organization by region then quickly narrows your focus. Read the company profiles for your targeted area and then consider: What type of spirits do you most enjoy? Which descriptions of unique products or flavor profiles caught your interest? Or maybe it's a business philosophy that impressed you, such as organic products or dedication to sustainable practices. Now you have a starting list of companies and products to explore. With the regional map in hand, it's time to plan some excursions.

Finally, make sure to check the Locator table, because the company profiles don't necessarily describe all the products they're making. Distilleries often have certain products in limited production, or single-barrel whiskey offerings, or other specialties they don't promote widely and may serve only at their tasting room. The Locator provides a complete list of product types in production and will help you discover these more hidden treasures.

Good luck! Discoveries at each stop will open paths of exploration in the remarkable realms of whiskey, vodka, gin, rum, agavé, brandy, liqueur, traditional styles, and spirits still being developed.

Let Us Hear From You

We welcome your suggestions about how to improve the *Guidebook*; comprehensive compilations like the *Guidebook* inevitably have mistakes and oversights. And as you visit tasting rooms and tour distilleries, tell us about your experiences. Send us an email or visit our website.

To order books or give us comments, visit CraftPublishing.net
Email: info@craftpublishing.net

PART 1
ARTICLES

WHISKEY & OTHER DISTILLED SPIRITS IN THE MOUNTAIN WEST

By Howell F. Wright

A LOT OF us grew up watching those B-Westerns, where a cowboy heads to the local saloon for a shot of red-eye to knock down the parched feeling gained from months on a cattle trail. In fact, old-time Denver or Santa Fe or Cheyenne could easily have been the setting for many of these movies.

Wyoming encampments like Lander, Riverton, McKinnon and Daniel were the spirit centers of fur-trappers and mountain-man rendezvous, with whiskey-laden mule trains trooping in each year for the event.

New Mexico was famous for "Taos Lightning," a wicked brew celebrated up and down the Rocky Mountains. This spirit was distilled by Simon Turley in Rio Hondo, New Mexico, starting around 1824. It had a wheat base and such legendary ingredients as pepper, tobacco and gunpowder.

Back in time in Blackhawk, Colorado

As late as 1910, there were more saloons in Denver than the total number of churches, schools, hospitals, libraries and banks combined. The city liked its drink.

Fast forward about a hundred years to March 4, 2004. That's when the team of George Stranahan, Jess Graber and Jake Norris founded Stranahan's Colorado Whiskey distillery—arguably opening the door for the craft distillery boom in Colorado and the Mountain West. Now we're seeing a spirits and saloon renaissance that could become even bigger than it was in the Old West. What began with one distillery in 2004 has grown, just in the tri-state area of Colorado, New Mexico and Wyoming, to just over one hundred times that number in 2018.

These new distillers are making a rich and diverse range of whiskeys, while also producing elegant and delicious vodkas and gins, rums and agavé spirits, with exciting flavors and standards of quality that can compete shoulder to shoulder with the big producers worldwide.

We now have more than 400 craft spirits produced in these three states, and we're delighted to spotlight more than 230 of their products in our featured profiles, with tasting notes and distilling information (pp. 57-197).

But that really is only where our adventure begins in understanding and enjoying the complexity and richness of craft spirits and how they are made.

Let's take a quick overflight and look closer at some specific areas in this rapidly expanding terrain.

WHAT ARE DISTILLED SPIRITS?

Distilled spirits are regulated in the United States by the Department of Treasury, Alcohol and Tobacco Tax and Trade Bureau (TTB), which classifies them in an array of 20 classes and about 100 types. The four most familiar classifications are: whisky (TTB uses this spelling), gin, rum and vodka. Brandy and liqueur also are specific classes of spirits.

To label their products as whiskey/whisky, gin, rum, vodka, or any of the other defined types of spirits, distillers must comply with the federal specifications. This

Whiskey or Whisky?

Of the big whiskey-exporting countries, Scotland, Canada and Japan use "whisky," while Ireland and the United States go with "whiskey." Both forms in that sense are correct, with the standard being a matter of tradition and culture.

In this book, we use the standard American spelling of whiskey. When discussing specific distillery spirits, we of course use the producer's own spelling for their specific whiskey products. Some prefer "whisky," especially when they align or produce their whiskey in the Scotch tradition.

does not mean that the great number of new distilleries simply are producing the same products. Craft distillers are developing an immense range of distinctive products within the general federal requirements through their skills as distillers, the ingredients they use, their specific equipment, and the way they age and finish their products. At the same time, growing numbers of craft spirits do

Fundamentals of Distillation

The basic concept of distilling is fairly simple. You need grain (or fruit or vegetable), yeast and water. First assemble a mash bill, which is your recipe, then cook the ingredients in a big pot called a mash tun. During the cooking process, starches are converted to sugar. Next move the resulting liquid or wort to a fermenting vessel, let it cool, then add a yeast strain (or several yeast strains) to begin the process of converting sugars to alcohol. The resulting fermentation product, called the wash, basically is a beer with five-to-six-percent alcohol by volume (ABV).

The beer then is moved to distillation, either in a pot still or column still, depending usually on what spirit you're producing. Vodka, gin and rum distillers generally use continuous distillation in a column still, while whiskey mainly is produced by craft distillers in a single small-batch process, often using a pot still system in which the alcohol normally goes through the system twice. The first distillation produces a strong, raw spirit. The second distillation produces a lighter, more flavorful spirit called new make or white dog. If the distiller didn't have a federal license, however, it's an illegal spirit known as moonshine—a label some brands apply, for marketing purposes, to their corn or white dog whiskey products.

depart from the standard classifications—and are designated "specialty spirits"—because there is more creativity coming from these folks than the standard federal definitions accommodate.

CRAFTING SPIRITS IN THE MOUNTAIN WEST

After touring distilleries in Scotland, I thought I understood distillation fairly well. The equipment there, as well as the fermenting and distilling techniques, were remarkably similar; the challenge was understanding the small differences that resulted in different products.

But in our own Wild West, there's no standard blueprint! Critical factors in the production and aging of spirits differ greatly not only from those in Scotland, or Kentucky and Tennessee, but from location to location in the region itself.

Consider just elevation—the highest distillery in Scotland is below the altitude of the lowest distillery in Colorado, New Mexico and Wyoming. Anyone who's ever tried to bake a cake at high altitude knows what I'm talking about. Even Kentucky or Tennessee techniques must be modified for our high-elevation Mountain West.

The concept of terroir—the combined influence of all local conditions—therefore is fundamental to the region's craft distillers. Soil, topography, climate, water, plants, quirks of the land, local yeast strains, barometric pressure and humidity—even the time of year—can affect characteristics of a distilled spirit, presenting complex challenges for every startup distillery. As you read each company's profile in the *Guidebook*, however, you'll note the many ways they have taken these challenges as opportunities.

The distinct characteristics of the Mountain West are applied as assets in making their products, celebrating the use of pure mountain water and quality local ingredients, often embodied in the concept of "grain to glass." Colorado distillers who purchase corn from the Southern Ute Indian Nation, Wyoming distillers who contract wheat from local farmers, and New Mexico distillers who gather local herbs and other botanicals—they all recognize the importance of terroir for the distinctive qualities of their products and have labored to make their products proudly local. Many distillers have gone an extra step by using only non-GMO grains, and some have committed to only organic grains for their certified organic spirits.

Small Batch

Most craft distillers have very small stills compared to the large producers in Kentucky, Tennessee and Scotland. When craft distillers start cooking a recipe in the mash tun, they run this batch of product through the entire process from beginning all the way to the white dog distillate at the end. After this small batch is ready for bottling or barrel maturation, they clean their equipment and start all over again on the next small batch.

Without a proven playbook, however, success for new distilleries ultimately has depended on trial and error, maybe in their barn or garage, that taught them, after great effort, how to make distinctive quality spirits in the Mountain West. Many have designed and built their own unique equipment, enabling them to experiment with off-the-map techniques and setting the stage for the exciting variety of products spotlighted in the *Guidebook*.

You can get a pretty good idea of how tough it is to start a distillery from advice given to David DeFazio of Wyoming Whiskey: "This will take you three times as long, cost three times as much, and be three times as hard as you think." In three of our chapters, the owners of Spirit Hound, Santa Fe Spirits, and Wyoming Whiskey share their experiences in starting and building successful distilleries (pp. 18-36).

WHISKEY

The craft spirits world is chock full of whiskey variety worthy of an entire course of study. But there are just five principal types— bourbon (corn), rye, wheat, malt (barley), and corn—plus the general class of whiskey, which is whiskey that does not meet the standards for any of the specific types of whiskey.

A small sample of whiskeys made in Colorado, New Mexico and Wyoming.

The first four types have the same specifications, just with a different principal grain—corn in bourbon, rye, wheat, and barley in malt—which must be at least 51 percent of the grain content used to make the whiskey. In their primary form, these whiskeys must be stored in charred new oak containers, typically barrels, for an unspecified period.

As Joe Elkins discusses in his article, "Maturing Whiskey in the West" (p. 37), aging in wood strongly affects the taste, smoothness and other qualities of the whiskey. Consequently, craft distillers typically store whiskey products in new oak barrels from three months to one year. Designation as a "straight" whiskey requires a minimum aging of two years.

The corn whiskey specification requires 80 percent corn in the mash, and barrel storage before bottling is not necessary. These specifications promote a clear, unaged spirit with a strong corn flavor unaltered by any form of charred oak. Light whiskey is another type, and it's stored in used or uncharred new oak barrels.

A comment about Scotch and Irish whiskey. Traditionally and by federal regulation, those names are reserved for products made in Scotland and Ireland. Does this mean that craft distillers in the U.S. can't make a good Scotch-style or Irish-style whiskey? No, it means the products simply are labeled as single-malt or Irish-style whiskey. More than a dozen Scotch-style whiskeys are produced in our three states. Colorado even has an Irish-style whiskey. Refer to the Locator table for the list of featured distilleries and the types of whiskey and other spirits they produce (p. vi).

VODKA

New craft distilleries typically start with vodka and gin as the first products they sell because they don't involve long-term maturation. Meanwhile, their whiskey ages in the barrel to achieve its desired quality. But quicker production doesn't mean unaged spirits must be bland, and some distillers choose to specialize in non-whiskey spirits.

Vodka can be distilled from any material, such as potatoes, beets, and grains like corn, wheat, rye, oats and barley; rice and even hemp are used by distillers in our three states. The distillate then is treated with charcoal or other materials "so as to be without distinctive character, aroma, taste or color." Many of the vodkas spotlighted in the *Guidebook* fit this description, but the federal definition of vodka as "without distinctive character" is a bit misleading. Vodkas often have distinctive flavor profiles because different ingredients and processing may produce subtle differences in character.

Vodkas also gain distinctive flavors through flavoring or infusion processes. These products actually are in a distinct federal classification: "Flavored Vodka." At a local package store I recently counted no less than nineteen different flavored vodkas, including honey, dill, cucumber, lavender, bacon, horseradish, jalapeño, watermelon, apricot, blueberry, chocolate, strawberry lemonade, black cherry and blood orange.

Flavored vodkas also differ in their flavoring method. As you read product descriptions in the *Guidebook* profiles, note whether a vodka is flavored with added natural or artificial ingredients, with natural flavor extracts, or infused with fresh fruits, botanicals or other natural ingredients. Flavorings may be added directly to the distilled vodka. Fruits or other natural ingredients may be immersed for some time in the vodka. Depending on the technique, the flavored vodka may be filtered or re-distilled.

GIN

Gin basically is vodka made with a characteristic flavor derived from juniper berries—most often Rocky Mountain junipers here in the Mountain West—and other botanicals. Craft distillers have hundreds of botanicals to choose from, including roots, herbs, dried fruits, barks, spices, nuts, and non-juniper berries. Many distilleries select their botanicals from plants specific to the region for distinctive flavor profiles.

On the world stage, there are four established types of gin with distinct characteristics: London Dry, which is most common, Old Tom, Genever and Plymouth. In the last dozen years, a new type of gin also has emerged, generally called New Western Dry Gin or American Gin. These gins keep juniper as a major ingredient but include other botanicals on an almost equal or even dominant basis, producing spirits with a broader range of aromas and flavor profiles. In addition to London Dry, this new style perfectly characterizes many gins made in our Mountain West states. But Genever and Old Tom styles, with recipes dating from the 18th century, also are produced here, offering intriguing new flavor experiences, I suspect, to many in our region.

RUM

Rum is distilled from fermented sugar cane juice, syrup, molasses, or other sugar cane by-products. Fermented sugar drinks may have been made in India and Pakistan as far back as 300 B.C., but the beginning of true rum distillation can be placed squarely at the feet of Christopher Columbus, who introduced sugar cane to what is now Haiti, the Dominican Republic and Barbados. The demand for sugar resulted in an excess of its molasses byproduct, which was dumped as waste until the 17th century when it began to be distilled into rum. It became extremely popular from Brazil to New England, with major commercial distilleries in New England. It truly is a New World product.

Rums are classed broadly as light, medium and dark. Light rums have mild flavor, or even vodka-like neutrality when triple distilled; dark rums, often from molasses and aged in heavily charred barrels, have stronger flavor; and the qualities of medium or amber rum fall between the light and dark varieties. Rum from sugar cane juice has a flavor profile ranging from earthy to herbal, while rum produced from molasses is more robust.

The quality of a rum depends on the sugar cane, which is affected by the soil and climate, the sugar components utilized (e.g., sugar cane juice vs molasses), the yeasts in fermentation, distillation methods, and how the spirit is aged—all of which invite experimentation by craft distillers.

Some manage the terroir of their products by carefully sourcing the sugar cane. For regional character, local sugar and roasted piñon nuts are being added during rum production. Distillers are creating their preferred flavor balance with

A sampler of vodkas, gins and rums made in Colorado, New Mexico and Wyoming.

blends of sugar cane juice and molasses in their mash. And some are using local sugar beets instead of cane sugar to make rum-like specialty spirits. You'll also find a wide variety spiced rums as you explore the *Guidebook*'s profiles of brands and their products.

AGAVÉ SPIRITS & TEQUILA

Tequila is a spirit distilled in Mexico in compliance with the laws and regulations of the Mexican Government from a fermented mash derived principally from the Agavé Tequilana Weber ("blue" variety). Agavé spirits can be distilled with the same ingredients, however, right in your home town—it just can't be labeled as tequila. Agavé spirit producers typically obtain the juice of blue agavé plants from Mexico but may also import the agavé itself and even specific yeasts to further replicate characteristics of Mexican tequila.

Some distillers also follow the traditional tequila styles: Blanco (white) must be bottled within sixty days of distillation; Reposado (rested) ages two to twelve months in oak casks, and Añejo is matured in oak barrels for one to three years.

ENJOYING YOUR COCKTAIL AND EATING, TOO

Beyond the tremendous diversity of individual products, the current renaissance in craft cocktails is greatly expanding ways to enjoy the distinctive characteristics of craft spirits. And it is not, of course, just about whiskey. Speakeasys and the broader cocktail culture serve more vodka than any other spirit, with gin, rum and other types of spirits having the spotlight in many favored drinks. In "Cocktails: A Marvelous Mingling" (p. 11), Lisa Hutchins helps us explore this remarkable re-emergence of finely crafted cocktails that is accompanying the rise in craft distilling.

The rich experience of craft spirits and cocktails is multiplied yet again when skillfully paired with food, whether in fine dining, outdoor barbeque or a casual gathering. "It's true," Master Chef Victor Matthews says in his article "A Match Made in Heaven" (p. 45). "Food can be good, and drinks can be good, but if you can properly combine the two they're so much better." Yet another wonderful dimension of craft spirits to be explored.

LET'S GET STARTED!

I hope this brief survey of the fascinating and expanding terrain of distilled spirits has helped you spot new areas to explore and provided some guideposts for your excursions.

If you relish discovery, start with the *Guidebook*'s product profiles and their regional maps to plan your tasting-room visits. Keep in mind that most of the more than 400 products being produced in the region are small-batch spirits that often are available first, and sometimes exclusively, at the distillery tasting rooms.

Get started and prepare to be amazed!

Howell F. Wright, Ed.D, a retired Colonel of Marines, has had a lifelong love of fine spirits and cocktails. A certified Whisky Ambassador, he has written blogs and newspaper articles about distilled spirits and managed multiple whiskey events. With a love also for the cowboy way of life, Howell and his wife, J'Ann, have taken leadership roles in the production of successful Western art shows and the management of the national award winning Rooftop Rodeo in Estes Park, Colorado, where they live.

COCKTAILS: A MARVELOUS MINGLING

By Lisa Hutchins

THERE'S A heady drink revolution taking place in restaurants, bars and distillery tasting rooms across the West. It's yet another golden age of cocktails—a scene that's vibrant, upstart and cutting edge. The movement is both old and new at the same time, reviving classics with craft spirits and sometimes reinventing them with a surprising blend of obscure botanicals, unique spirits and heritage techniques.

With craft, every element of the cocktail is taken into consideration and elevated, using high-quality ingredients. Craft cocktails are created with much care to give the customer a more satisfying and beautiful drink. They're not just "something from the bar."

THE ORIGINAL HEALTH DRINK

Spirit aficionados will be happy (or amused) to learn that cocktails actually started out as medicinal treatments. While healers administered herbal treatments with flowers, leaves, bark and roots in wine or other fermented liquids for thousands of years, distilled spirits arose within the last two millennia. Evidence points to ninth-century work by Arab scientists in designing the alembic pot still. By the twelfth-century, distillation had made its way from the Middle East to Europe. And with the introduction of distilled spirits, herbal tonics or curatives could be preserved and made even more potent—evolving into what we now call bitters.

Throughout the Renaissance, bitters were prescribed for nearly every conceivable malady: digestive issues, headache, sea sickness, depression, poor circulation. By the 18th century, bitters dissolved in Canary wine had become popular, especially in colonial America. From there it was a small step to putting prescribed bitters into a mixture of spirits, water and sugar to increase palatability. And there we have the cocktail.

And the origin of the word? There are at least a dozen guesses as to how the name came about. Depending on the source, "cocktail" could have come from a French egg cup, a Yankee innkeeper thief, rooster tail feathers, a lovely Latina, high-stepping horses, a ceramic jar or even an old beer mix called cock ale.

Whatever the word's origin, during cocktail's infancy the pharmacist was more apt to dispense drugs and medical advice than a doctor. In fact, since doctors commanded a much higher fee, the apothecary essentially functioned as a low-wage doctor to the common man. The most famous example is Antoine Amédée Peychaud, a Creole apothecary in New Orleans who created the Sazerac. In this way apothecaries became the first mixologists, working to prepare more palatable potions for their patients.

Along with bitters, some of the most well-known cocktails and cocktail ingredients began as medicinals. Vermouth and absinthe, distilled from wormwood, were used for stomach issues. Peychaud's Sazarac—one of the earliest recorded cocktails—was said to combat intestinal parasites. Aquavit was considered an antibacterial (and in the Middle Ages, even reputed to bring back the dead when poured down the throat). Ginger beer warded off seasickness. Quinine, made from cinchona bark, was the only botanical known to fight malaria. The British took it via the Gin and Tonic. The French looked to Dubonnet and Amer Picon for their treatment, while the Italians relied on Campari.

By the mid-1800s, cocktails had moved away from health and into recreational drinking. Cocktail mixing ascended to the heights of high art through master bartenders such as Jerry Thomas, today considered the father of mixology. Thomas was famous for a legion of cocktail-related exploits, but especially for his signature Blue

Blazer cocktail, a streak of fiery lit spirits he'd toss from glass to glass. The bar and its cocktails became a truly American invention, exported to the most sophisticated spots overseas.

COCKTAILS ON THE FRONTIER

Although the Old West was replete with rugged cowboys knocking back shots of "whiskey straight," frontier men liked their cocktails too. A julep called the Hailstorm—made with Taos Lightning, sugar, wild mint and ice gathered from the roof

A Hiccup Cure

Like the beginning of making an Old Fashioned. Put two drops of bitters on a sugar cube to eat.

after hailstorms—was served at Bent's Fort on the Santa Fe Trail (near present-day La Junta, CO) in the 1830s and 40s. According to restaurateur Holly Arnold Kinney of The Fort Restaurant in Morrison, Colorado, the Hailstorm is the oldest known cocktail in the state.

HAILSTORM JULEP

- 3 oz bourbon, scotch or cognac
- 2 tsp confectioners' sugar
- 2 sprigs fresh mint

Crush ice to fill one wide-mouthed pint Mason jar or julep cup. Mix the alcohol, sugar and mint in the jar before filling with ice. Secure the lid and shake vigorously. The ice will bruise the mint in order to release its flavor. Once well shaken, remove the lid, drink from the jar, and enjoy!
(*Courtesy of The Fort Restaurant, Morrison, Colorado*)

Shrubs—a type of drink made with fruit or berry juice, sugar, alcohol and vinegar—were a popular summertime thirst quencher on the Trail. At other establishments there was the Muleskinner, a mixture of whiskey and blackberry liqueur, and Cactus Wine, a blend of tequila and peyote tea. Santa Fe hotels, offering the only sophisticated lodging during early frontier days, provided drinks such as the Martinez gin cocktail, Tom and Jerry and rum punch.

Prohibition in 1920 almost dealt the cocktail a knockout blow in the U.S., but by the post-war years, cocktails came roaring back. Even so, the 1950s and early '60s were more about quantity than quality, with three-martini lunches, cocktail parties and two-for-one Happy Hours becoming the norm. There were "lady's drinks" and "men's drinks." Women sipped Grasshoppers or Pink Squirrels, and men stuck with robust favorites like the Manhattan and Tom Collins. Then in the late 1960s, cocktails hit the skids once again, officially out of fashion and tagged as part of The Establishment.

It was Dale DeGroff, cocktail's savior and author of *The Craft of the Cocktail*, who brought the cocktail back from the shadows around the turn of the century. DeGroff, or King Cocktail, as he's known, may be the grand old man of mixology today, but it's largely young people who've picked up the ball and run with it right off the field.

> **Make Clear Ice**
> The way to enjoy craft spirits.
> Start with distilled water. Bring the water to a boil. Let cool while covered to keep out dust or particles. Bring to a boil a second time and let cool as before. Pour it into an ice cube tray. Cover tray with plastic wrap and freeze.

A REBIRTH

The people creating craft cocktails come from all walks, but share a common quest to "do things better" with spirits. Their independent stance takes form in distinctive, handmade, locally-sourced and even non-GMO or organic spirits and liquors. Unlike the cocktail lifestyle a couple of generations ago, the new movement emphasizes fresh, high-quality ingredients rather than tired, over-sweetened and mass-produced compounds. Craft distilleries typically maintain one of the best destinations for craft cocktails in their own tasting rooms, where they mix small-batch spirits with local botanicals, hand-squeezed juices and house-made bitters and syrups. Throughout the tri-state region, craft cocktails beckon to everyone from cowboys to skiers to tourists to urban hipsters.

Colorado: With the fourth-highest number of craft distilleries in the nation, Colorado is moving up fast as a leader in craft spirits and cocktails, edging out bigger neighbors like Texas. Stephen Gould, co-founder of Golden Moon Distillery and its speakeasy in Golden, Colorado, attributes this rise to "the current food scene. People care about where their food comes from. They're more discerning about what they put in their bodies." Ryan White of Devil's Head Distillery in Englewood, Colorado, concurs: "Locavores are willing to pay more for quality and care, and to support local economies." In addition to the nearly eighty tasting rooms of the spirit producers in Colorado, there are dozens of standout bars across the state for craft cocktails, including Denver speakeasy William & Graham (named America's best cocktail bar), Boulder's Bitter Bar, The Wobbly Olive in Colorado Springs, and Aspen's Hooch Craft Cocktail Bar.

New Mexico: The New Mexico cocktail scene is strongest in the northern part of the state, according to Natalie Bovis, founder of both The Liquid Muse and the annual New Mexico Cocktails & Culture Festival. "A lot of really impressive bartenders are developing their skills and making a splash in the craft cocktail scene here," she says. Bovis adds that, since culinary art is one of the state's biggest industries, festival seminars demonstrating the latest mixology techniques are heavily attended.

SILVER COIN MARGARITA

- 1-1/2 oz silver (blanco) tequila
- 3/4 oz fresh-squeezed lime juice
- 3/4 oz orange liqueur
- 1 bar spoon agave nectar
- Garnish: lime wheel

Rim a rocks glass with a mixture of salt, sugar and red chili powder. Fill with ice, set aside. Pour all ingredients into a cocktail shaker, shake well, and strain over the fresh ice in the glass. Garnish with a lime wheel.

New Mexico has historically been famous for the Paloma cocktail, while the apple cider-based Chimayó cocktail is considered by aficionados to be the state's official cocktail. But if there's a people's choice for New Mexico, it has to be the Margarita. Although the Margarita was reputedly created south of the border, New Mexicans have enthusiastically adopted the drink as their own.

Wyoming: While the Wyoming craft cocktail scene is still in its infancy, there are top spots like The Rose in Jackson Hole (voted one of America's top cocktail bars by *Food & Wine*) that represent the pinnacle of cocktail culture. For much of the state, "vodka base is the name of the game," says Amber Pollock, co-owner of Backwards Distilling in Mills, Wyoming. Wyomingites appreciate the introduction of fresh juices and, for now, lean toward lighter flavor profiles, with Bloody Marys and Moscow Mules being especially popular.

INDIAN PAINTBRUSH

- 2 oz bourbon or blended bourbon*
- 1 oz Benedictine-like liqueur**
- 1 oz fresh lemon juice
- 2 dashes bitters (pine or Angostura)
- 6 raspberries
- 5 sage leaves
- 5 basil leaves
- 3 oz ginger beer

Lemon twist, mint and evergreen sprigs for garnish

Muddle raspberries, sage, and basil in a Boston shaker. Add remaining ingredients except the ginger beer. Shake hard for 20 seconds with ample ice to extract the fruit and herb flavors. Loosely strain into a Collins glass or small mason jar 2/3 full of cracked ice. (Seeds and bits sneak through, adding texture and color.) Top with the 3 oz of ginger beer. Twist lemon peel over the drink and then garnish with the twist, a full sprig of mint and some pine or spruce greenery.

Suggested: Backwards American Whiskey* and Koltiska KO 90**

(Courtesy of mixologist Jeremy Hugus as an ode to Wyoming state flower and terroir.)

Jeremy Hugus, a Casper attorney and cocktail columnist for the Casper *Star-Tribune*, is helping Wyomingites broaden their horizons. "Be open minded," Hugus advises. "Drink what you like, but be willing to try new things." Pollack concurs, noting the Backwards Distilling staff see their job as helping customers become more adventuresome. "We're pushing the envelope a little bit," she says. "Gently. But we're pushing it."

BRINGING IT BACK

Today's distillers and mixologists are mining the old and obscure, sometimes pouring through antique texts in search of forgotten recipes that are proving extremely popular with the cutting-edge crowd. One of these is Crème de Violette. Virtually impossible to find until a few years ago, the liqueur was distilled in the 19th century for its supposed cancer-fighting properties—then all but lost to time. Resurrected by Gould and now made at Golden Moon (located appropriately enough on Violet Street), the distillery uses a botanical called blue violet. "It's an amazing seller," Gould reports. "Not just here but all over the world. Our Crème de Violette has a beautiful violet note, but with a lot more complexity than other violet liqueurs."

Similarly, Devil's Head Distillery started with aquavit, a Scandinavian spirit with caraway seeds, now outselling both their vodka and gin combined. The number one cocktail at White's bar is an Old-Fashioned, in which they use barrel-aged aquavit to give it a fresh spin. "We call it Notes of a Dirty Old Man," he quips.

From the bar scene, Sujib Timilsina, bar manager for the Wapiti Pub in Estes Park, Colorado—at the east entrance to Rocky Mountain National Park—reports, "We have more than four million visitors a year in Estes from all fifty states and around the world. When they come here, they want to drink something Coloradan—something they can't find back home." Even as recently as five years ago, Timilsina adds, nobody at their bar asked for craft cocktails. "Now, kids in their mid-twenties routinely request them."

With the current cocktail renaissance and corresponding rise of craft spirits, never has cocktail quality been so good. Bartenders and craft distillers are relishing the spirit of innovation and bringing cocktails along with them—reviving what was lost, honoring the old, upgrading the tired and creating the new. The hour of the cocktail has truly arrived.

Lisa Hutchins is a professional writer and a contributing editor for this *Guidebook*. She blogs about her passions at lisahutchinswriter.com, especially wildlife, nature, and the spiritual path. She's been a staff writer for *Colorado Life* magazine, managed and edited an Audubon chapter newsletter, and owned a backyard birdfeeding store. Currently she's developing her photography skills and working on a children's book from her home in Estes Park, Colorado.

HAVE THE RIGHT STUFF?
STARTING SPIRIT HOUND

By Craig Engelhorn

STARTING A beverage alcohol distillery is no casual endeavor. Approaches vary, from those who intend to produce large quantities to those who choose to fill a neighborhood need as the "local distillery," and those who distill all their products from the start to those who begin by finishing and bottling bulk spirits purchased from established producers.

In 2011, four friends in Lyons—Wayne Anderson, Neil Sullivan, Matt Rooney and I—started Spirit Hound Distillers, with the intent to produce whiskey from the ground up using Colorado grain, hand-made distilling equipment and full-size oak barrels. We chose from the outset to produce "straight" whiskey, with the requirement that the whiskey barrel-age at least two years. In the interim, we planned to produce some clear spirits to generate revenue in the first few years of operation while waiting for the whiskey to mature.

FINDING YOUR PLACE

Small distillers benefit greatly from direct retail sales in their own tasting rooms. Spirit Hound's tasting room is co-located with the distillery in Lyons, Colorado, on U.S. Highway 36, the major route to Rocky Mountain National Park only twenty-five miles away. As they say: location, location, location. Thanks to the tasting room's prime location, Spirit Hound enjoys a very busy summer season, exposing its products to consumers from all over the world.

Lyons is a small town, however, landlocked by mountains and unbuildable "open space," meaning suitable locations are rare. So when a large metal building directly on Highway 36 became available (previously the Red Hill Motorcycle Werx), my partners and I immediately began negotiating a purchase.

During the ensuing eighteen months of negotiations, we also began construction at an alternate location in Longmont, in the back lot of partner Matt Rooney's veterinary hospital. We filed the

Spirit Hound federal permit application during this time, using the Longmont location as the plant address. Then, in February 2012, we reached an agreement to purchase the Red Hill location in Lyons. At that point, we halted the Longmont construction and re-filed the federal permit application paperwork with the Lyons address. Fortunately, perseverance and an eye toward the goal of an outstanding location in Lyons worked out, and Spirit Hound now enjoys a somewhat enviable location.

Charting a Course

While we were acquiring property and submitting permit applications, we spent significant time trying to divine the direction, approach and feel for the products that Spirit Hound would make. Luckily I had experience in beverage alcohol production as the original brewer for Oskar Blues in Lyons; I had even contacted the Colorado Liquor Enforcement Division back in 2000 with hopes of adding whiskey production to the Oskar Blues lineup. Unfortunately, the hurdles back then were just too large for a small brewpub to tackle, or else Oskar Blues might have been the first Colorado distillery in modern times.

My experience making beer and fermenting malted barley led to Spirit Hound's whiskey approach—start with an all-malt wash, lauter (rinse to remove the grain), and ferment in a closed sanitary environment before distilling two times in simple pot stills.

Next step was forging an early relationship with the Colorado Malting Company, which at the time was the only maltster in Colorado. The recipe for Spirit Hound Malt Whisky calls for a portion of "peat-smoked" malt, which after many conversations with Colorado Malting Company was added to their product line in time for the seventh barrel of Spirit Hound Whisky. As a result, Spirit Hound Straight Malt Whisky became a 100-percent Colorado product.

Developing the Business

Raising capital and allocating its use are critical components of any company startup, and Spirit Hound was no exception. The banking world isn't keen on financing a venture that plans to build inventory for several years before selling it for revenue. Since we

weren't able to self-finance the startup, we turned to an idea similar to wine futures: "pre-sold" barrels of whiskey.

Most of the purchasers were friends and family. But several were liquor stores, as well as in-state and out-of-state distributors. This program was extremely successful, to the extent that people still ask if they can get in on a barrel purchase.

A major advantage of this approach was that there was no loss of equity for Spirit Hound partners, because the capital raised was based on actual product, albeit future product, not a share in the company. A second benefit was building a network of people who were highly vested in our success. A third advantage involved the liquor stores that bought into the program—they made sure the whiskey went on their shelves, and they were very happy to promote Spirit Hound and sell our other products to help grow the brand and make their whiskey investment more lucrative.

BUILDING THE PHYSICAL PLANT

As Spirit Hound's direction solidified and startup capital arrived, we focused on the required physical plant and equipment. A model that heavily relies on sweat equity and a do-it-yourself attitude pervades all aspects of the Spirit Hound production area. Rather than go for a turnkey approach with new equipment and the associated ease and expense, we relied on a combination of home-made, scavenged, used and repurposed equipment.

First, we constructed a small pot/reflux still from plumbing parts and a used beer keg. After obtaining quotes from Vendome,

Christian Carle, Holstein, and the like, I (fortunately or unfortunately) opened my big fat mouth and said, "If you guys buy me some tools and some copper, I'll just build one." That's how we ended up building the custom pot still ourselves.

The spirit still turned out to be a one-of-a-kind work of art. Fully made of copper and modeled from shapes reminiscent of stills found in Scotland (Spirit Hound is following the malt whisky tradition after all), my partners and I made it entirely ourselves. The tools, custom jigs, and sheer amount of effort and learning required might suggest that this isn't an approach for the faint of heart. However, many small distillers craft their own equipment, so doing it yourself cannot be discounted as a legitimate approach. And arguably, if serendipitously, the shape of Spirit Hound's pot still contributes to a unique, generally sweet and very favorable distillate.

Handmade Pot Still

The still began as a two-dimensional CAD drawing and fabrication stayed close to the original design, as seen in photo. All stills at Spirit Hound are steam-fired, and the spirit still is heated by a copper coil in the bottom of the still. This system may be easy to fabricate but isn't suitable for distilling on grain.

We used a CAD program to lay out the physical plant, including tank positions, floor drains, etc. I was able to take the physical dimensions of the stills, six newly acquired fermenters, as well as assumed footprints for future equipment, and design a floor plan for efficient use of the existing space. We employed an architect and two engineering firms to ensure that the buildout met current building codes, the steam system was adequately specified, and the plans could be approved. Construction ensued, which mostly entailed cutting in trench drains and plumbing for steam, as well as building a separate fire-walled building to the west as a boiler room. We fully believe in keeping any flame sources far away from the production area!

STEP BY STEP

We phased capital improvements and the introduction of equipment as it could be afforded. This meant that our company reinvested profits over several years to incrementally improve the production area. The initial equipment, for example, included one 15-gallon gin still, one 150-gallon pot still, and six 1000-gallon fermenters. The fermenters were scored at an incredible bargain from a defunct Rock Bottom Brewery.

In those early days, we had a deal with a nearby brewery, Upslope Brewing in Boulder, to use their mash tun and kettle to brew wash, which was hauled in a converted bulk milk tank back to the distillery, where it was pumped into a fermenter. After about a year of operation this way, we installed a mash tun and kettle, saving the trips to Upslope. The mash tun and kettle are repurposed equipment from a Kraft Foods cheese plant in Wisconsin, sized to fill 750 gallons of wash into a fermenter in a single brew.

After that, Steve Williams, lead distiller for Spirit Hound, and I designed, built and installed a stripping still. The stripping still sits atop an 800-gallon repurposed stainless-steel tank that was purchased for scrap price. The copper hat and tube in-shell condenser were then designed and built in house, continuing our do-it-yourself attitude. Over the years, Spirit Hound continues to design and build new equipment and improvements as needs and cash flow dictate. Current and upcoming projects include a new gin still, a mash plow to clean out the mash tun, and adding barrel storage space.

STAYING THE COURSE

All new small distilleries face obstacles to startup and growth. One formidable set of hurdles is understanding and complying with federal regulations and taxes, along with state and local requirements, for distilled spirits manufacturing. For Spirit Hound, understanding federal regulations is a continuous process, and I review them on an annual basis to stay fresh and gain better understanding.

Another "complication" that could have been devastating for Spirit Hound was the Great Flood of 2013, which decimated the town of Lyons. At just ten-months old, Spirit Hound had produced exactly six barrels of whiskey and a single barrel of rum when the flood hit our building, leaving it inundated by the St. Vrain River for a day and a half.

Suddenly the focus changed from producing spirits to removing mud and rebuilding—a process that took several months, crippled cash flow and delayed the next whiskey barrel by nearly eight months. While it's rare for a natural disaster to crash through a small distillery, it's a lesson in diligent disaster planning, as well as making sure that insurance policies

Flooded September 2013

are written with proper coverage. Since then we all joke about tying a boat to the building year-round.

With the flood squarely in the rear-view mirror, our focus returned to producing quality products and building our brand's reputation. Before the whiskey was ready to bottle, a small product lineup kept the cash flow alive and subsidized further whiskey production. During those years we sold gin, a rum, a sambuca and the occasional specialty, as well as an unaged version of whiskey known as "white dog."

Spirit Hound Gin, produced with a gin basket in a small still that seemingly runs on a continuous basis, features local Rocky Mountain Juniper (juniperis scopulorum) and several other botanicals. It's a smooth, balanced gin that is popular in Colorado, especially along the Front Range. Part of its success has been an agreement with our customers: I tell them, "If you bring me a four-finger bag of juniper berries, I'll give you a gin drink in trade." As a result, Spirit Hound has a fresh supply of junipers and actively engages customers in the process of making our gin by bringing them right into the Spirit Hound family. Alongside the gin, Spirit Hound now sells its Straight Malt Whisky, as well as the rum, sambuca, and white dog. A four-year rye and a bourbon whiskey are in the pipeline. (See Spirit Hound profile, p. 88.)

DISTRIBUTION TO BIGGER MARKETS

The distillery tasting room is a great cash cow, especially with sales at retail prices, but distributing product into the outside market gives a much larger potential sales footprint, and our initial plan was to move into the marketplace as soon as product was available.

Wayne Anderson, our Director of Business Development, has an excellent bio in beverage alcohol sales and distribution as the former Oskar Blues sales director during their explosive growth and "canned" revolution of beer. As such, Wayne's relationships with liquor stores and distributors throughout the state and beyond made it possible for Spirit Hound to get products onto store shelves quickly. After self-distributing for about six months, we entered into an agreement in May 2013 with Beverage Distributors (which became Breakthru Beverage).

Spirit Hound products are widely available throughout the Colorado Front Range and generally available statewide. In keeping with a philosophy of filling out the "backyard" first and growing in a controlled fashion, Spirit Hound just entered the Kansas and Nebraska markets in 2017. While those are relatively small markets, they're nearby and we're lucky to have a number of friends and family there who provide "boots on the ground" support. Next up is Texas in the Spring 2018. We expect that the very large Texas market will help continue our 30-percent average annual growth.

MANAGING EXPANSION

Spirit Hound has ample production capacity for the next few years of growth, but right now we're tight on storage space. We plan to soon expand the Lyons facility—mainly to increase storage, but also to gain a footprint for more efficient processing and bottling areas, and generally to just have some breathing room.

The tasting room will gain from the expansion as well, with increased parking to serve more customers on busy days and during events. Spirit Hound utilizes its backyard as an outdoor cocktail garden, and it's very popular in the summer. The Town of Lyons plans to install a foot-, bike-, and golf-cart path immediately behind the Spirit Hound patio, which will allow easy and safe off-street access to the distillery.

COLORADO PROUD

As I said at the beginning, starting a beverage alcohol distillery is no casual act. Start the process by developing an idea into a tangible plan, including a clear understanding of philosophy and both short- and long-range goals. Next, it's essential to find a suitable location and come up with a reasonable financial plan that clearly documents initial and sustainable funding.

Obviously, you have to know (or be prepared to learn) how to make products that will be part of your line. And somewhere in the mix, you need to make or acquire all the equipment for distillation and develop a plan for maturation and bottling.

It may not be easy, but starting and building a distillery brings great satisfaction and a feeling of accomplishment. To be a part of a Colorado industry that's growing at such a rapid rate, and where the definition of quality distilled spirits is changing almost daily, gives meaning to the term Colorado Proud.

Craig Engelhorn, co-owner and head distiller at Spirit Hound, grew up in Nebraska as a science enthusiast, going on to earn an electrical engineering degree and MS in computer science. In 1996, after a rewarding career at AT&T Bell Labs, he moved to Lyons, where he later helped Oskar Blues install a brewery with their new restaurant and as their first brewer. When not in his distillery, Craig enjoys working on old cars and scanning the heavens with his homebuilt telescopes.

UNDER THE APPLE TREE
HOW IT HAPPENED AT SANTA FE SPIRITS

By Colin Keegan

MY ORIGINAL career was as an architect and right about the time the bottom fell out of the Santa Fe housing market, I had designed a house in nearby Tesuque on property that had an apple orchard. The project fell apart, but my wife and I liked the location. So we bought the property, built a house, and started tending the orchard.

Each year I made apple juice, invited friends over for a day of harvesting and pressing apples, then sent people home with more apple juice than they could drink. Hard-pressed, you might say, to find a way of using all that apple juice, I started making hard cider—and that led to apple brandy.

In early 2010, there was little work for a high-end, private home architect, so I decided to apply for the required federal and state licensing, buy a building and still, and turn my hobby into a fun part-time job!

ESTABLISHING THE DISTILLERY

Founded by European colonists, Santa Fe is the second-oldest colonial city in the United States. As such, it has rather strict zoning laws. Fortunately, just as I was in the market for a distilling building, the city had rezoned property south of town for manufacturing and industry. We found a site and today our distillery remains in that original building, though over the years we've expanded by opening our on-site tasting room in 2011; adding a new warehouse and bottling area in 2012; adding additional storage space, offices and a dedicated barrel aging room in 2013, as well as an off-site tasting room in downtown Santa Fe. In 2016 we built a full rickhouse, yet again increasing storage space and turning our distillery tasting room into a beautiful event space.

DEVELOPING THE PRODUCT LINE

From the outset my goal was to make an American single-malt whiskey, as well as apple brandy. But they both need to age, so we (now grown big enough to be "we," not "I") created a line of clear spirits to take to market. Silver Coyote, an unaged whiskey, was our first product to market, followed quickly by Expedition Vodka and Wheeler's Gin. Santa Fe Apple Brandy went to market in 2013.

Our Colkegan Single Malt Whiskey was released in 2014 and has become our leading product with the greatest demand, particularly outside of New Mexico. We have also added two specialty liqueurs: Atapiño, a piñon nut and pine sap-infused whiskey, and Slow Burn, a smoked gin liqueur.

Santa Fe Spirits Distillery

We've expanded our Colkegan line with Colkegan Cask Strength and Colkegan Apple Brandy Barrel Finished (a mouthful, both to say and to drink), which is our flagship Colkegan that rests an additional six months to a year in a used apple brandy barrel. [See Santa Fe Spirits profile and products, p. 188.]

COMPLIANCE CHALLENGES

Each product had to be formulated, tested and able to be produced in a consistent way, and that was the easy part! Compliance—that is, label approval, formula approval, filing and receiving patents, etc.—was the real challenge.

When we started out there were fewer craft distilleries in the country than there are now, and the system was set up for large-scale companies. In larger companies there are entire departments devoted to compliance. In contrast, a small startup usually has about three people to do every job, but there's also a greater sense of accomplishment at the end of the day—or so we tell ourselves.

DEFINING OUR BRAND

While developing our product line, we decided it was important for our products to reflect the unique feel and terroir of the American Southwest. To that end, all our spirits are made with indigenous Southwest ingredients that can be found within fifty miles of the distillery. Our Colkegan Single Malt whiskey is made in the style of Scotch, but rather than peat-smoked malt we use mesquite-smoked, providing a unique flavor profile. Our gin has among its ingredients sage and cholla cactus blossoms. And our Atapiño Liqueur was created by Johnny Jeffery, inspired by the scents that surrounded him on a trail run in the Santa Fe mountains.

MANAGING GROWTH AND DISTRIBUTION

As we've grown from a local Santa Fe distillery to a New Mexico distillery to a Southwest regional company, we've had to make many adjustments to keep up with demand and ensure we have the right people on our team. Craft distilling is fairly new to New Mexico, so there aren't a lot of industry-experienced people at hand. That means each member of our staff comes from a different background and has a different perspective. To have all of us sitting around a table together brainstorming is truly exciting.

Making our mark now in the national arena has become our biggest challenge yet. Certainly we're no longer local or regional when selling in New York, and getting our footing and figuring out our niche in larger markets takes a different approach.

Sales and distribution are complicated and sometimes frustrating challenges, taking enormous resources not normally found in a small business. Our product does best being hand sold to the consumer, the restaurant or the liquor store, but the current U.S. three-tier system is distributor-driven. The distributors in turn are driven by the big suppliers.

Our go-to-market approach therefore continually changes, and there's no one approach that works across all markets. Our sales and marketing team must constantly be on their toes, keeping up with trends, dreaming up new ways to get our products into the hands of the consumer. As with all small businesses, the team is key. We've been fortunate to put together a great team at Santa Fe Spirits. We know we're going to succeed.

TASTING ROOMS

We have the advantage of two tasting rooms—one at the distillery and one in the trendy downtown Railyard District—where we're able to sell our products, deliver our message, and serve cocktails created with our spirits (or any spirits produced in New Mexico). They make a huge difference in our ability to reach the public.

Our distillery tasting room is geared more toward education and is primarily used for spirits classes, tours and tastings, and more recently has become an event space. Our downtown location, on

Downtown Tasting Room

the other hand, is a great venue for tasting the very best cocktails, all made with New Mexico distilled spirits. Situated in the busiest part of Santa Fe, this cozy tasting room sees a lot more traffic. It's also one of the few high-end cocktail establishments in our city.

WORKING TOGETHER AS AN INDUSTRY

In 2016, Santa Fe Spirits and four other New Mexico distilleries formed the New Mexico Distillers Guild, which has expanded to twelve participating distilleries. The guild works primarily to grow and sustain craft distilling in the state and educate the public about what craft distilling really is.

As a guild we have a stronger voice in industry legislation, and we can participate in national conversations with other groups such as the American Craft Spirits Association (ACSA). Since I'm always active in any endeavor that promotes our business, I'm currently an ACSA board member, which I've found to be fulfilling, educational and successful. It's organizations like these that can establish artisan distilling within the beverage industry and help our industry reach the status that American wine producers and breweries have already achieved.

Some ask whether starting a guild gives away ground to our competitors. The answer is no. As a group we're very helpful and congenial with each other. There's not a day without a call or email from a colleague asking for information or sharing it. We're truly a band of brothers working toward a common goal.

Since Santa Fe Spirits began, the number of craft distilleries in the United States has expanded from 200 to more than 2,000—and more start up every year. Yet the biggest challenge to our industry isn't the increase in competition, but the outdated three-tier sales system that currently dominates the market. As a group, both within the state as New Mexico Distillers Guild and nationally as American Craft Spirits Association, we're striving to overcome our challenges. Our confidence in beneficial change comes from the public because they want better and more diversified spirits, just as they did before us with wine and beer—and what the public wants, the market will deliver.

ACCOMPLISHMENTS AND ONGOING CHALLENGES

Even with our serendipitous beginnings, starting and sustaining a distillery isn't for the faint of heart—or for the idle farmer looking for a fun way to use a harvest. Some afternoons we end up slumped around the kitchen table with barely enough strength to lift our tea cups. At times like this everyone asks me: "Colin, tell me again: why did you start a distillery?"

The myriad challenges often seem Sisyphean: Each state has different compliance laws. Big Liquor has a tight grip on distribution. We're too small for large distributors, yet small distributors have their own survival challenges. With products that needs to age, we're constantly planning for years down the road, not knowing if there are any years down the road. It would be easy to throw our hands in the air and walk away.

But then we look at our achievements. In eight short years we've grown from one employee to eight full-timers and four part-timers. Our facility has expanded from 2,500 square feet to over 11,000 square feet. We have a product range of five spirits and two liqueurs, and distribution in eleven states and three countries. We've received national recognition for all of our spirits, and growth is more than twenty-five percent a year.

That's enough to get us back to work, sleeves rolled up and ready to face new challenges.

Colin Keegan, owner and head distiller of Santa Fe Spirits, moved to Santa Fe a few years after leaving his native England in 1990. He continued a successful architecture career across the Southwest until the severe 2008 economic downturn. That event prompted him to concentrate on his dream of building a distillery where he could produce his own versions of traditional Scotch and brandy.

THE MAKING OF A WYOMING DISTILLERY

By David F. DeFazio

THE CONCEPT of Wyoming Whiskey was born in spring 2006, at the dawn of the craft spirits era. Brad Mead, a fourth-generation Jackson cattle rancher, and his wife Kate decided to make bourbon in the wake of a Hot Springs County land purchase. The purchase was designed to allow winter cattle some grazing land far away from the elk herds that descend on Jackson during deep snow. Who would have thought separating cattle from elk would lead to the birth of a whiskey brand? But the land seemed to point the way.

DEVELOPING A PLAN

At the time, Brad, Kate and I weren't aware of the term "craft spirits." We were just three Wyoming mountain attorneys who knew nothing about making whiskey but plenty about drinking it, and decided to make bourbon without a playbook. So when tasked with the job of figuring out how to make bourbon, my first step was looking to the birthplace of American whiskey. I planned a trip to Bardstown, Kentucky.

The first contact came that fall during the Kentucky Bourbon Festival with Max Shapira, past president of Heaven Hill Distillery. As head of the largest family-owned bourbon distillery in the country, Max had a kindly yet clear message for us: "Don't do it. It will take you three times as long, cost three times as much, and be three times as hard as you think." Despite the eventual truth of his words, we pressed on, working first with Lincoln Henderson, a legend in the industry who educated us on traditional whiskey's history, art and components. Next, Vendome Copper and Brass designed a continuous still system for us, downsized from the ones typically found in Bourbon County.

Up until then the project seemed easy. Even though copper was selling at historically high rates, we had a still maker, a rough sketch of the distillery and land in the middle of the Wyoming grain belt. But who was going to put it all together? Neither Brad,

Kate nor I had the aptitude for bourbon making, and Lincoln had long ago moved on from day-to-day distillery management.

It was a call to Rob Sherman at Vendome that helped form our future. Within a month he rang back to announce he'd found our guy. He was Master Distiller Steve Nally, who'd learned the trade during thirty-three years at Maker's Mark. Since his time at Maker's Mark, Steve had been on the sidelines and was ready to get back in the game. Wyoming Whiskey gladly handed him the ball.

Constructing a Facility (and its pitfalls)

By then our distillery construction was underway. But Wyoming was in a natural-resources extraction boom. Contractors were in short supply, forcing us to import an out-of-state general contractor running multiple jobs with no pride in his work. Not only that, it was difficult to find a construction workforce when oil field wages were higher than anywhere else. The project quickly fell behind schedule. Concrete was poured incorrectly and had to be re-poured. The few installed iron posts remained bare for months and resembled dead trees stripped of their limbs by wildfire. It was depressing. Faced with unacceptably slow progress, we at last fired the contractor and construction then sat idle until we could locate a new contractor in nearby Cody.

At that point the future of Wyoming Whiskey was already in question. The project had been set back an entire year, with much of our money wasted on the first contractor. Were it not for the Mead resiliency and my stubborn conviction to succeed, Wyoming Whiskey might have died then and there. Max Shapira's prophesy echoed in my thoughts.

Luckily our new contractor, Dale Cowan, proved to be excellent, creating for us a smaller-scale version of a classic Kentucky bourbon trail distillery. He and his fully-staffed crew renewed our enthusiasm to make America's next great bourbon, completing construction in June 2009--a year later than originally planned, but ready for us to flip the switch on Wyoming's first legal distillery.

The Regulatory Environment

Given Wyoming's short tenure as a state and its focus on live-stock and fossil fuels, one might think that non-existent alcohol manufacturing laws might have presented a major obstacle. Happily, this wasn't the case. Wyoming granted us a manufacturer's license after a nominal fee and relatively easy application. That certificate, License Number One, reflected our status as the first legal distillery in the state. However, because the craft distilling industry had been non-existent until then, Wyoming Whiskey still had to help develop the body of law that would eventually govern the sampling and sale of our products.

Permitting Tasting Rooms

While the Wyoming beer and wine industries had already generated laws that allowed the sale of products at producer-owned "satellite" locations, no such legislative permission existed for distillers. We began the process of contacting state legislators to lobby for equal treatment for our industry. What we found was, while the Wyoming Retail Liquor Association wasn't opposed to one satellite per distillery, they were staunchly opposed to three satellite locations as allowed for the wine industry.

Since retailer support was essential for our success, we saw no reason to push for more than one satellite. In the end the legislators in Cheyenne overwhelmingly agreed, but not before we spent a lot of time and effort assuring the success of the bill. Lesson: Don't underestimate the time and effort needed to change a law.

Lessons in Developing Products

Production began at last on July 4, 2009, ushering in a relatively smooth period. Steve experimented with a number of yeast strains, along with the few that Lincoln recommended. We ultimately settled on two that would be used in tandem to produce our family of whiskeys.

We lined up Brent and Sherri Rageth of Byron, Wyoming, to grow our non-GMO grain. And after initially getting lesser-quality barrels from a Kentucky cooperage, we eventually sourced reliable barrels from Independent Stave in Lebanon, Missouri. Always line up competing vendors when you're new to the industry. Another lesson: Never assume a vendor is quoting the best price or providing highest quality.

Our production schedule quickly went from a single-batch, six-day production schedule to a double-batch, four-day one, improving efficiency and output. But what we should have recognized is that whiskey coming off the still during the first phase of production won't be your finest. It takes a while to dial in fermentation environments, distillation and condenser temperatures, ideal entry proof and plenty of other details. When it came time to begin bottling, those imperfections contributed to a less-than-ideal bourbon. The whiskey off the still at the outset should be considered a loss until the process is fully dialed in.

DEFINING A BRAND

Early on we decided to create a custom bottle with an embossed WYOMING on the front and WHISKEY on the back. Luckily we began the design process early enough to allow for plenty of thought, followed by an even longer production schedule. Creating a bottle from scratch presents a number of challenges. Round, oval or square? Short or tall? Thick glass or bubbled? Gradually the vision took shape, differences were resolved, and after a few months it was time to work with our manufacturer.

Our volume wasn't high enough for reasonable pricing from an American company, which led us to a Mexican company. We learned the concept of timeliness is honored differently by different cultures. Delivery dates for the preliminary and final molds were repeatedly extended, forcing us to issue weekly reminders. While the Mexican manufacturer never missed a deadline, they never delivered as requested. Another factor to keep in mind is customs.

Our goal was to have glass at the border at least a month in advance to accommodate import issues. It was only by chance that we received our first glass shipment in time to meet our launch date of December 1, 2012.

PLANS VS. REALITY

We learned you can never have too much storage. Pallets of glass take up lots of space, as does cased whiskey ready to be shipped. Our bottling building quickly needed expansion to house a truckload of double-stacked pallets. We also added room for additional large dumping tanks, needed to accommodate production

increases, and the considerable space required for barrel aging.

It was overly optimistic of us to think that three years of aging would be long enough for our flagship Small Batch Bourbon. During the maturation process there's great demand for barrel storage, meaning considerable cost over time for warehouse construction and storage. And with a name like Wyoming Whiskey, there wasn't going to be any cash flow from clear spirits while our whiskey aged.

In our experience, four years of aging is a minimum. In the end we settled on five years for our core product and longer for select other products. Full capitalization is critical to a new company that won't have a product to sell for five or more years. Remember, like Max said, this is going to cost three times as much as you think.

THE DISTRIBUTION STRUGGLE

Although we're fortunate to work with a marketing company, 77 Ventures, that tells our story like no other, by far the biggest difficulty we've faced is out-of-state distribution. An entire book could be devoted to this topic. We've been very successful selling Wyoming Whiskey in-state. The home field advantage, combined with a healthy tourist traffic, has resulted in robust sales numbers. But local success doesn't necessarily travel across state lines.

A new brand needs a devoted body to grow, especially when aligned with a large distributor. We learned this the hard way when we first stepped out of Wyoming in 2013. Out-of-state sales were insignificant compared to our Wyoming successes, and sales expenses were something we simply didn't expect. In the end we decided to strategically hire and place salespeople where we saw the most potential. With a few exceptions, we've moved away from large distributors, instead working with moderately-sized ones that are sincerely interested in helping us build our brand.

LOOKING FORWARD

Despite stepping on a few rakes along the way, Wyoming Whiskey has enjoyed great success since its 2012 launch. We're now sold in over 30 states, offer a family of six different whiskies and gained the attention of experts and consumers alike. In 2016 our Barrel Strength Bourbon was honored as one of the top ten whiskies world-wide by Whisky Advocate, and in 2017 Esquire magazine named us the top family-owned distillery in the U.S. making its own products, as well as the number two craft distillery overall. Since that first spark of an idea twelve years ago, we've enjoyed tremendous progress. Wyoming Whiskey continues to grow and the future looks bright.

[See Wyoming Whiskey profile and product descriptions, p. 196.]

David DeFazio is a founder and COO of Wyoming Whiskey. From Delmar in upstate New York, he was lured west in 1996 to Jackson Hole, where he's managed DeFazio Law, a four-attorney law firm on the Jackson Town Square. When not attending to whiskey or practicing law, he relishes days fishing mountain streams, skiing and cheering the New York Yankees.

MATURING WHISKEY IN THE WEST
TRADITION & INNOVATION IN CRAFT DISTILLING

By Joe T. Elkins

B Y AGING whiskey in wooden barrels or casks, what begins as a clear, fiery liquid is transformed by time inside the barrel into a complex, smooth and pleasant amber liquid. Oxygen in the air, acids in the whiskey and from the wood, and other wood compounds interact chemically to form new flavors over time, giving whiskey its unique and much desired flavor.

But traditional barrel aging takes years to mature the whiskey. This creates a financial dilemma for young, small distilleries, which constitute the bulk of distilleries in Colorado and other western states.

In the last decade, there's been a revival of craft distilling, with the majority of new distilleries making whiskey. There are now at least eighty distilleries in Colorado, and most have opened since 2012. With so many new distilleries making whiskey, there's both a need and an economic incentive to produce good whiskey in shorter periods of time. These new distilleries are mainly small operations that can't afford to put whiskey in barrels and wait years before the product can be bottled and sold. Many of them are looking to science to understand barrel-aging chemistry and reverse-engineer the process to get results much more quickly using some very clever methods.

Before examining these newer methods, we'll review the traditional aging techniques for whiskey that the innovators are attempting to match in quality.

THE BASIC WHISKEY

Whiskey straight from the still goes by various names—white lightning, white dog, moonshine. Today, true moonshine is primarily produced from sugar, and although it may have some other flavor adjunct such as corn or fruit, it is not whiskey. But because moonshine is clear and colorless, many unaged whiskeys are colloquially called the same name. "White dog" is perhaps the most correct and consistently-used name in the distilling industry because it refers specifically to clear, unaged whiskey.

Newly distilled, unaged whiskey often is described as "hot" or strong. It takes some time and persistence to appreciate newly-distilled white dog. One of the properties that changes most by maturing whiskey is its relative "heat." Whiskey that's matured for thirty days has a noticeable smoothness compared to freshly-distilled whiskey. This is equally true for clear whiskey stored in glass vessels and isn't a function of exposure to wood or atmosphere.

In the U.S., only corn whiskey can be labeled and sold as whiskey without aging in wood casks. Bourbon, Tennessee whiskey, malt and rye must all be aged in new, charred wooden casks to be sold as whiskey.

TRADITIONAL METHODS OF BUILDING COMPLEXITY

Whiskey usually is stored in wooden casks on racks inside warehouses or rickhouses. The permeability of wood allows whiskey to interact with the atmosphere, leading to tasty esters— the goal of whiskey maturation. Esters are the flavor compounds we experience that aren't directly associated with wood or grain. Flavors such as banana, coconut and pineapple are the result of acid esterification during fermentation. Banana-tasting esters, such as those found in Tennessee whiskey, are the result of yeast, while vanilla esters are the result of wood. All these esters make each brand, and indeed each barrel, of whiskey distinct. The real trick is finding the ones you like most—and discovering that can take years. Thank goodness for the side benefit of whiskey consumption during such a diligent quest!

While storing whiskey in barrels may seem straightforward, the outcome can be quite varied depending on the wood type and how it's originally cured; how the wood is treated with flame or heat, which is gauged as "toast" and "char" levels; the warehouse microclimate and how it may vary over time; the barrel's previous use (if any); and the proportion of blended product.

One of the most striking changes is color. Barrel-matured whiskey can range from deep brownish amber, commonly associated with bourbon, to pale yellowish gold like some blended Scotches. This color range is entirely the result of the tannins that develop from temperatures the wood has been exposed to, as well as the barrel's previous uses.

Scotch matured in traditional rickhouse

Barrel agitation also can have a notable effect. During the 19th century, whiskey in wooden casks that was transported by pack animal to the western slope of the Appalachias—at that time, the American frontier—was reported to have a smoother taste than its newly-distilled counterpart. Similarly, bourbon transported in wooden barrels down the Ohio and Mississippi Rivers was valued as smoother, despite being in barrels only a few months. To that end, Jefferson Bourbon now has dozens of bourbon barrels on the decks of shipping vessels, allowing them to age at sea. The resulting whiskey is indeed smooth and contains a hint of iodine flavor from months at sea.

THE ROLE OF CLIMATE

Hundreds of thousands of barrels of corn-based whiskey such as Jim Beam (bourbon) or Jack Daniel's (Tennessee whiskey) are made from majority-corn grain bills, stored in new charred American white oak barrels, and aged typically from three to six years in multi-story warehouses throughout Tennessee, Kentucky and Indiana—states that have remarkably similar climates with substantial seasonal temperature variation. These commonalities produce spirits that are much alike in color and flavor, being a dark brownish amber and having an overall sweet flavor with notes of ripe fruit and vanilla.

American whiskeys that are aged in new charred oak barrels can be stored too long, resulting in an overly woody, "tannic" whiskey. Distillers using small barrels, particularly in the hot and dry American West, should be extra careful if their storage warehouses aren't temperature- and humidity-controlled. Large temperature swings can accelerate interaction with the wood. And hot dry conditions accelerate the loss of product through evaporation—poetically referred to as "the angel's share"—and also increase the relative proportions of bitter acids.

Scotch, by comparison, ages mostly in used whiskey barrels, primarily from the U.S., and in very humid and cold conditions. Used barrels have been substantially depleted of organic acids that result from the original charring or toasting of the wood, so it can take three-times longer for Scotch, when matured in these used barrels, to extract the same amount of tannins as with new barrels.

The combination of used barrels, a wet and cool climate, and smaller variations in those conditions requires Scotch to be aged for much longer periods of time, usually ten years and more. But the result is a beverage that's unmatched, making Scotch perhaps the most admired whiskey in the world.

ADDITIONAL FINISHING

In the past five years, an "extra-matured" process, or finishing, has become popular. This usually involves harvesting four-year-old whiskey from the original barrels and placing it in freshly-emptied barrels that contained another beverage—most commonly wine, sherry or port, but sometimes also rum, tequila or barrel-aged beer. The sugars and esters from these liquids add to the complexity of the finished whiskey, resulting in a diverse, complex taste profile that's growing in popularity. Jameson Caskmates, Glenmorangie Quinta Ruban and Angel's Envy employ this aging method.

INNOVATIVE MATURATION METHODS

Traditional methods of maturing whiskey set the standard of quality that new methods are judged by. So why not just use the proven methods? Some new companies do make that choice and have a business plan, including long-term financing, that allows for the delays that traditional aging methods involve. The innovators, however, have a variety of motivations in developing new techniques. Getting their products to market sooner certainly is a leading motivation. Reducing the costs of maintaining large rick-houses is another advantage. Most whiskey is aged in oak barrels; some new methods make it much easier to use many other woods that may not be as suitable to barrel fabrication. This opens additional horizons for crafting new characteristics into whiskey and other distilled spirits. New methods also can be more ecologically sustainable than traditional aging in new oak barrels by greatly reducing the demand for harvesting new trees. And innovators continue searching for other benefits as they explore the mechanisms for maturing distilled spirits.

ACCELERATED AGING

A variety of accelerated mellowing techniques have been used to improve the flavor of alcoholic beverages. One way is aging on wood chips. The distiller fills a mesh bag with dried or toasted wood chips and places the bag into a container of white dog. Depending on treatment of the wood chips, the whiskey can achieve the desired color and taste in a matter of weeks or even days. After that the chips may be discarded or blended with new chips, while the bag is reused and put back into the next batch of whiskey.

The benefits include a super-fast production time, adequate-to-excellent color change, rapid infusion of wood-derived compounds, and low overhead costs since chips are very inexpensive compared to a wooden cask. The down side, though, is insufficient oxidation of acids—meaning a more limited range of esters. Whiskeys using wood-chip mellowing are "young" tasting and commonly lack the fullness, depth, complexity and smoothness common among barrel-aged whiskeys. Also, any mistakes made in the process can really stand out.

In another technique, Cleveland Whiskey in Ohio ages whiskey for six months in barrels and then puts the whiskey-filled barrels into stainless-steel pressurized tanks. In this method the spirit is agitated for about a week, passing through the pores of the barrel within the tank.

ALTERNATIVE BARREL DESIGN

Another company has redefined the casks for aging distilled spirits. Squarrel Barrel of Fort Collins, Colorado, uses a square-shaped, stainless-steel framework with flat wooden staves. The staves in the containers are easily exchanged—without the skills of a trained barrel cooper—once they're depleted of the wood-derived compounds that are quickly extracted by white whiskey. The staves are cut with numerous grooves, increasing the wood-to-whiskey surface area, and wood varieties that aren't suitable for making conventional wooden casks can be milled into flat replacement Squarrel staves, enabling new whiskey-wood combinations that previously were impractical. The square design also means a tighter storage arrangement because distilleries can fit more square barrels into an area than conventional round casks.

Inside a Squarrel Barrel

The technology still is in prototype, with dozens being tested in a variety of applications across the craft beverage industry, but early results are promising. Ten-gallon Squarrels have produced very nice whiskeys in as little as forty days. The Squarrel also allows producers to use conventional names such as bourbon, malt and rye, since the federal government doesn't define the shape of a barrel or its construction details. The Squarrel initially costs three to four times more than a conventional barrel of equal size, but replacement staves are about one-third to one-quarter the cost of a conventional barrel. Cost savings are seen in the second and third use of the Squarrel.

SONIC AND ULTRASONIC TECHNOLOGY

Hertzbier is a technology that speeds up the whiskey-wood interaction using sound waves from a sonic transducer inside the whiskey-filled barrel to agitate the liquid, forcing the whiskey to move through the wooden pores. This increases the rate of oxidation reactions of acids and decreases the time it takes to form esters.

The Hertzbier method has the advantage of satisfying aging standards for bourbon, malt, and rye—all requiring the use of a barrel in their production as defined by the federal government. Other technologies that don't use a barrel cannot apply those specific terms to the whiskey, even if the white dog employs a bourbon, malt or rye mash bill.

Ultrasonic wave treatment to accelerate mellowing creates an environment where chemical polymers break into sub-particles and then recombine into a different compound for the final product. While only recently applied to whiskey, ultrasonic treatment has been applied for several decades to change the chemical and sensory profiles of other alcoholic beverages, including coffee liqueurs, sake, corn wine and, most notably, to accelerate Spanish brandy mellowing and to make high-ester rums.

Lost Spirits Distillery in Los Angeles has developed a process using ultrasonic waves, heat and short wavelength light. These treatments degrade the wood, without charring it, and drive oxidation and esterification to create high-ester rums in just a week. They currently have pilot projects with their patented technology at less than a dozen craft distilleries across the U.S. The resulting rum is impressive, with gas chromatography-mass spectrometry (GC-MS) analyses showing compound similarities to thirty-year-old barrel-aged rum after just a few weeks.

Another company, Terressentia Corporation in South Carolina, is exploring accelerated mellowing with TerrePURE, which employs ultrasonic energy, oxygen and heat to remove impurities that negatively affect the taste.

Given the success of ultrasonic wave treatments to improve the flavor of other alcoholic beverages, this technique has promise in producing whiskey comparable to barrel-mellowed products. At Elkins Distilling Company, we use both wood chip maceration and ultrasonic wave treatment to speed up the extraction of ethanol soluble wood compounds for a smooth, young whiskey with light oak notes. [See Elkins Distilling profile and products, p. 72.]

Distilleries applying accelerated mellowing typically treat their methods as proprietary technology and publicize little or nothing about their approaches. Additional publicly-available research on acceleration techniques can make important contributions to the field.

CONSUMER DEMAND AND INNOVATION

The excitement surrounding advances in accelerated mellowing of whiskey will continue for years to come as the world demand for whiskey grows. In 2017, the U.S. distilled beverage industry sold $120 billion of product. By comparison, U.S. domestic crude oil production was worth $160 billion. That same year in the United Kingdom, whiskey accounted for £25 billion in sales.

With middle-class societies in China, India and Russia clamoring for more whiskey, producers will struggle to meet that demand, particularly if conventional barrel aging for two to six years is the only production route for commercially-competitive whiskey. The potential to have competitive whiskey after only weeks of aging therefore will continue to drive development of the accelerated aging technologies.

Producing craft whiskey is about taking chances, following a passion, opening businesses, innovating and adding a unique contribution to the whiskey legacy. No matter the equipment variations, feed stock grains, production methods, yeast strains, distiller cuts—the resulting whiskey is celebrated locally for its distinctive character, and new maturation techniques are expanding their role in this creative and rapidly growing industry. It's an exciting time to be part of the craft distilling revival in the U.S.

 **Joe T. Elkins**, Ph.D., co-founder and head distiller at Elkins Distilling Co. in Estes Park, Colorado, is an avid outdoorsman and an award-winning professor in the Earth and Atmospheric Sciences Department at the University of Northern Colorado. After moving to Colorado in 2008, he has been making whiskey since 2010. His research includes the role of climate, geomorphology and geochemistry in the production of alcoholic beverages and the science of accelerated mellowing of alcoholic beverages.

MATCHES MADE IN HEAVEN
WHISKEY & FOOD ADVENTURES

By Master Chef Victor Matthews

I'M STILL a country boy. I've studied for advanced degrees and been an American culinary ambassador, but no letter pile after my name is going to take away the days of sitting by the still running a batch of moonshine whiskey in the holler between grandpa's house and Junior Johnson's place keeping the dogs quiet with hushpuppies (yes, that's where the name came from) while the volunteer fire department practiced backwoods structure fires just a few hundred yards away.

Speaking of the fire department, they never found grandpa's still. Got close but never did, even though each Saturday we ate their barbecue chicken at the fire station. Everybody did; it was about the best in the county, with a light vinegar sauce rather than heavy ketchup stuff, because that goes better with 'shine, and we'll talk more about that in a bit.

Bourbon & Homemade Ranch Dressing: If you've never had real homemade ranch on crispy ice-cold lettuce, you should know there's no substitute. A week ago, I was having one of those days and was not real pleased with life right then. I hadn't eaten all day and was feeling what my family calls "hangry." So, I dropped into the local roadhouse. The cook there is *good* and they carry my whiskey.

"Bourbon and coke tall, ranch salad," I said. *Ahhh . . .* I called my wife to tell her a joke and she said, "You sound like a completely different person." "Of course," I replied. "Bourbon and homemade ranch dressing solve everything."

It's true. Food can be good, and drinks can be good, but if you can properly combine the two, they're so much better. We call this a good pairing, but doing it correctly with whiskey is harder than with beer or wine.

Spirits tend to be high in alcohol, at least forty percent, and many whiskeys even higher. This creates burn and blows palates while providing complexity that's hard to unveil. For the great masters searching for depth, nuance and innovation, whiskey pairing has become a focal point for cutting-edge bars and restaurants. Using cocktails provides a way to add back some of those organic elements that go missing during spirit distillation, and doing this wisely can lead to the best pairings in the world. It can be as easy as matching two elements, as in bourbon-pecan ice cream or bourbon and lemon chicken. In this article we'll look at the fun side of the puzzle, as well as the higher-end, fine-dining side.

REGIONAL PAIRINGS

The idea of regional pairings revolves around using a locale's history and culture for both food and drink to arrive at a safe combination. If a whiskey and a dish were developed in the same area, it's a good guess they might work together. The most direct and somewhat bizarre example is with Scotch and haggis, where the overbearing qualities of Scotch are subdued by the insanity of haggis, a savory pudding made of sheep's organs, thereby putting the guest in a state of awe that supersedes any flavor profiling.

We've mentioned already the Southern pairing of corn-based moonshine and barbecue. Non-whiskey examples are Jamaican rum and curried goat, or tequila and tacos. My favorite high-end versions of that idea combine fresh lime margaritas with ceviche or pair saketinis with sushi, matching both flavors and regions. Let's look more closely at some great examples of historic regional whiskey pairings.

Early American Cuisine & Whiskey: To begin, we go to eighteenth-century New England. A combination of Scottish and Irish immigrants in the region provided distilling knowledge, which blended with British and German cultures that brought beer knowhow. All this came together with an overabundance of Dutch rye crops and, voila, rye whiskey was born.

Rye was blended with some of the malted barley used for beer, providing not only needed enzymes but some recognizable background flavors for British-Americans. Remember that during this time the spirit was still clear; barrels had not yet been used in aging. If you cannot locate a clear rye whiskey, which is rare these days, simply use the youngest one you can find or just try your favorite rye. It's the floral lightness of the rye, combined with early American history, that gives us this pairing.

LOBSTER EN CROÛTE & AMERICAN RYE

Rye is floral but also a bit spicy. The acids and alcohol content react quite well with richer, fattier foods, breaking down the richness and cleansing the palate (think dry French wine paired with brie). Here a cream-based dish is called for. Also, as you know from clam chowder, the cream stew is a staple of New England and the early colonies.

The lightness of white or young rye partners with seafood, provided the seafood is substantial. That brings us to the greatest seafood of America, the lobster, which we'll prepare with cream and a buttery pastry. The acids will be bright and subdued while the floral rye will pull out the herbs, making the dish even better.

For this dish, however, you'll need a one-and-a-half to two-pound live lobster per couple (or a one-pounder for an individual) as well as three jumbo shrimps per person. This, of course, is an elegant five-star dish, and if you want to do something similar on a

lower scale, substitute two pounds of bone-in fish or use all shrimp as we'll indicate in the recipe steps. Also, if you need a lower alcohol percentage or want a non-whiskey for the mixed drink, use lemon drop or margarita concepts, so you're incorporating alcoholic beverages that work with lobster.

Basic Recipe: To dispatch a live lobster quickly, insert a knife in the head crease and cut quickly forward to split the head. You also can put it in the freezer; cold-blooded creatures do not feel temperature in the same way and just slow down until they die. Or use the standard boiling salted-water method. Up to you, but you need to get out the tail, claw, and the rest of the meat, then set aside. For the stock, chop up the shell, including all the goodies inside.

Lobster stock: In a small heavy-bottomed pot, cook a half-cup mixture of onions, celery and carrots in butter until soft. Add the lobster shell and innards as well as any shrimp shells you have, plus a couple bay leaves and a little thyme and black pepper. Next add one cup white wine and a splash of rye, plus 1-1/2 cups of water. Bring to a boil and cook uncovered for an hour until reduced to 3/4 cup of liquid. Filter out the solids, keeping your strong, wonderful lobster stock.

For the fish option, make the stock with its bones and head; for all-shrimp variant, use the shells—with both options replace 1 cup of water with clam juice.

Once you have your stock, finely dice a quarter-cup of onion and mince a tablespoon of garlic. Also prepare a couple tablespoons of fine-diced celery and carrots. In a good-sized pan, sauté the onions and veggies in butter, then add the garlic and two bay leaves. Sprinkle only enough flour to absorb the butter and make a tiny amount of roux, not much. Add the lobster meat (or the fish and shrimp, for those options) and shrimp, all diced in large pieces. Cook just one minute to get it started but NOT fully cooked. Add your stock and a half-cup heavy cream. Taste and adjust salt and white pepper to make it perfect.

Take this creamy, chunky love full of lobster (or fish or shrimp) and shrimp and divide into individual tureens to near the top, but keep liquid somewhat lower. Top each with puff pastry (you will probably want to buy that pre-made from the store; check the frozen section). You can fashion a decoration on the pastry if you like, and use egg wash to make it shiny. We call this *en croûte*. (If you're not familiar with *en croûte* and need more guidance, look it up on YouTube; it's a common chef technique.) Follow the baking instructions for the *en croûte;* typically 400-450°F for 10-15 minutes, but only long enough for it to rise and brown.

Diablo Variation: Use the rye in a Bloody Mary cocktail and add tomatoes, paprika, sriracha and spices to make a kicked-up arabbiata sauce. Use this sauce as your stock in the recipe and reduce the amount of heavy cream. Sort of the opposite of the creamy classic version, but either way it's delicious.

Backwoods Classics

As opposed to the more sophisticated pairing above, we'll look now at rustic put-togethers from the backwoods that use moonshine, corn whiskey, bounce, lightly-aged whiskey and even the rare muscadine brandy—in general, all the old-school drinks and recipes from Appalachia and related areas. There are so many wonderful combinations within this realm, but in general think of Southern fried food. The acids in alcoholic beverages cut into those fats, creating a wonderful balance. Dishes like the greens and beans of the South have a rich mouthfeel that works well with most liquor.

For those who'd rather mix the spirits, remember the South is king of simple cocktails. For instance, any liquor goes into sweet tea. Also consider lemonade. You can give it some fancy bartender name, but lemonade makes a great, easy cocktail. My personal favorite is the julep. Mint and sugar go so well with whiskey, and don't forget the mule concept (drinks that involve ginger ale or ginger beer, citrus juice and any number of base liquors), because whiskey mules are even better than the original vodka-based concoctions.

But perhaps the most important elements in a rustic pairing involve wood. The flavors of toasted, charred wood in whiskey have obvious cross-connections with smoked foods, and any smoked food is sure to find a perfect whiskey partner. Smoked fish and oysters go with lighter whiskeys, just as champagne goes with caviar. Before we get to the never-before-published barbecue recipe from my hometown fire department, let me suggest a few more pairings.

With lighter whiskeys such as white dog or unaged offerings, try wood-plank salmon—you can find recipes for that all over the internet. For whiskeys that are a little heavier, I like bacon anything, but especially bacon-wrapped pork chops or steaks, or a personal favorite, bacon and jalapeno mac-and-cheese.

Around my house, heavier bourbons and aged whiskeys get chocolate-and-ice-cream pairings, or else become part of another local favorite: candied pecans and caramel-swirled ice cream over a warm bourbon brownie, served with either straight bourbon or warm bourbon coffee. Don't forget how good most whiskeys are with dessert and coffee; they stand out in the after-dinner course. But let's get to the special firehouse barbeque chicken that we saluted at the beginning.

WILES COUNTY BARBEQUE CHICKEN & MOONSHINE PALMERS

Although this chicken is legendary, initially it's going to seem a little odd to those outside of the Carolinas. Vinegar-based barbecue often confuses people, but it's a lighter way to deal with chicken or pork, so there are good culinary reasons for it.

Basic Recipe: We start with a brine because conventional basting could wash away the surface seasoning that we'll be using. Dissolve one cup salt in a gallon of water and submerge a whole chicken in this brine overnight in the refrigerator. The next day when you're ready, remove the chicken, dry it and rub it down with any simple oil in preparation for cooking. (Note: Brining is sensitive to elevation; longer above 6500 feet and less time below 4000 feet—just a few hours at sea level.)

If possible, build a wood fire, using the coals and wood to create a combination of smoke and heat. If this isn't possible, use a higher-heat smoker or regular grill—but if you must use a grill, employ the lid and be careful not to burn the chicken. The idea behind this technique is a fusion of smoking and grilling, although if you have to choose, lean toward the smoked side.

Open the chicken and either leave it whole and flattened (what chefs call spatchcocked), or just cut the bird in half. Next, throw

the chicken on the fire or smoker and baste every five to ten minutes with the special Carolina sauce below. We call this "mopping" because the fire department used cotton mops to coat the chicken continuously, but you can use a pastry brush or any other technique.

Carolina Sauce: The secret to the chicken is slow cooking and lots of basting with the legendary Carolina barbecue sauce. Heat together 1 qt apple cider vinegar, 1 cup apple juice, 1/2 cup sugar, 2 Tbsp salt, 2 Tbsp red pepper flakes, 2 Tbsp black pepper, 2 lbs butter.

This sauce is related to a vinaigrette, or even a *beurre blanc*. Butter makes the dish rich and delicious, while mellowing the pepper and spices. Also, since you'll be basting the uncooked meat for a while and may cross contaminate, please *reserve half the sauce* for pouring over the finished chicken. Depending on whether you're grilling or smoking, this could take as little as half an hour or up to two hours. When the chicken is finished, pour some of the reserved sauce over the bird and serve it with a little on the side to dip. Mix the sauce up fresh each time you use it.

Side Dishes: With this barbeque, I like potato salad (generally the mustard-and-onion type) and coleslaw (usually "pink," meaning red wine vinegar and mayo). But the whiskey pairing here must be moonshine-based. If you want to use aged 'shine or even a bourbon, that's fine, but make your spirits American and as country as possible. Our favorite barbecue drink is either sweet tea, lemonade or a combination of the two called an Arnold Palmer. We take it a step further with our Moonshine Palmer: Mix two ounces of 'shine with four ounces lemonade and four ounces sweet tea. Pour over ice in a tall glass. Enjoy!

BACK TO THE HIGH END

Pairings for fine dining can be made from either direction: you can match the whiskey to the food or start with a favorite cocktail—from whiskey sours and mint juleps to your own version of old fashioneds, mules and Sazerac—and create a dish around it. The list is endless. We'll use a high-end Manhattan version with this recipe.

The classic Manhattan consists of whiskey, sweet vermouth, bitters and a cherry. But here, let's upgrade it. Start with a good, aged, smooth bourbon. Makers or Woodford would work, but I prefer an artisanal choice for this pairing, if possible. One hint about sweet vermouth is to treat it more like wine than liquor—that means keeping it cold and using it fresh. As to the bitters, I prefer homemade; alternatively, use a combination of cherry and orange bitters or find one that's fruit-based. The maraschino cherry needs to be high-end as well, such as Luxardo or another fine brand.

Manhattan Recipe: 2 oz great bourbon; 1 oz fresh, cold Italian sweet vermouth; 1 oz cherry brandy; 2 dashes quality bitters; 2 dashes maraschino cherry juice. Shake well and serve up in a chilled martini glass with a best-quality maraschino cherry.

What could we possibly pair with such a fabulous cocktail? Why, duck of course. The cherry theme—a natural pairing with duck—appears throughout the cocktail, the dish and its accompaniments.

THE ULTIMATE MANHATTAN WITH ROASTED DUCK

If you've never roasted a duck before, have no fear. It's easier than a chicken and this recipe is great.

Basic Recipe: Get a good duck from your favorite market. It will likely be frozen, so thaw it in the refrigerator. Trim some of the excess fat off the back side. Remove any innards and cut shallow crosshatch cuts into the breast fat, being careful to cut only the fat, not the meat. This will allow fat to drain so the skin can become crispy.

Next, thin out some honey with a small amount of water and rub the whole duck down with the honey-water mixture so the spices will stick. Season liberally with kosher salt, black pepper, dried thyme, garlic powder and onion powder. Place in a roasting pan set to hold a good amount of rendered fat and roast at 400°F for an hour, if cooking ahead. If serving immediately, use 425°F.

At the end of the roasting time, the duck should be golden brown and the skin crispy. Remove it from the oven and let it rest. If you'll be serving it later, you can split the duck in half at this point and cool it, then reheat in a medium oven (350°- 375°F) for 15 minutes when it's time to serve. If the reheated skin is not crispy, warm it in a hot oven (375°- 400°F) to crisp the skin.

Now let's look at the sauce and spoonbread.

Spoonbread is an old-school dish like savory bread pudding. It relates a bit to British pudding or what the Pilgrims called popovers, which can be substituted here if you like. But to make the spoonbread, you'll need some dry old bread, any kind, just not too weird like rye or flavored bread. Crumble the dry bread or rough chop into chunks and place in a mixing bowl. You'll bake the mixture in a pan 2"- 3" deep and 9"- 10" on a side. You need enough bread to fill the pan loosely to the top *twice*.

Spoonbread Mixture: Mix 1 pt heavy cream, 1 pt whole milk, 6 eggs, 1 Tbsp salt, 1 Tbsp white pepper, 2 cups dried cherries, 1 Tbsp dried thyme, 1 Tbsp Better Than Bouillon chicken base. Whisk thoroughly.

Soak the bread with the liquid mixture. It should be thoroughly moistened, neither sopping wet nor dry. Adjust as needed with either a little more milk or a little more bread. Let the bread-soaked mixture sit for an hour to absorb. Coarser bread takes more liquid and soaking time.

Now, butter your pan heavily and pack it tight with the soaked bread and cherry mixture. Spread it evenly in the pan. It should reach near the top. Pack it down and bake it at 350°F for about 1 hour, or until it's tall and proud. It will be somewhat similar in consistency to a soufflé, but not extremely so.

After the spoonbread rests briefly, it's ready to serve. I like to cut a 4"- 5" circle and lift it out. If you don't have a circle mold, serve the bread as a square, like lasagna. Lean the crispy, delicious duck up against the spoonbread on each plate and finish with the following sauce. You can cook the sauce while the spoonbread is in the oven.

Cherry Sauce: In a saucepan, place 2 cups water, 2 Tbsp Better Than Bouillon chicken base, 1 tsp white pepper, 1 cup cherry brandy, 1 cup cherry juice, 1/2 cup dried cherries. Simmer the sauce for an hour and thicken with a cornstarch slurry. You should have a delicious, shiny red sauce that tastes like chicken and cherry.

Spread the cherry sauce on the plate in front of the duck and spoonbread. If you pour the sauce over the duck, it can de-crisp the skin, so a nice puddle under the duck will do. You should be able to see the sauce up front in the presentation on the plate, because the duck stands up against the spoonbread. That's the side you serve the guest, we call it six o'clock. I usually garnish with a nice bouquet of thyme—flowering if possible—behind the duck in the spoonbread. Beautiful and delicious.

LAST THOUGHTS

As you can see, pairing food and whiskey has delightful possibilities. On one level it's cutting edge, sometimes challenging and extremely popular among the elite diners of the world. Yet you can easily reproduce these dishes at home.

Decide first if you're going to start with the drink or the food. Once you've determined that, you can build off the basic pairing strategies. Try to match regions or flavors, and try to have a theme, whether it's downhome country or fine dining.

Sometimes your idea starts with a wonderful whiskey you want to pour. Are you going to use it straight or make a cocktail? Once you decide, taste it and look for flavors to match. Smokiness is easy to pair with smoked foods, and caramel or sweetness is great with more acidic foods. Remember, the higher the alcohol content the more palate burn you get, so try to lower that impact. Cask strength is best for sipping but more difficult for pairing.

Don't be afraid to experiment and taste things to get ideas; and remember that these creations usually start out as an amusing dream. There are no hard and fast rules—just have fun and enjoy! I filled a watermelon with moonshine last summer and let it sit in the refrigerator for a week. Then I cut up the melon, diced it nicely and mixed it with sushi-grade tuna for a moonshine tartare.

The sky's the limit! See you out there . . . and keep savoring your whiskey joyfully and responsibly.

[See Black Bear Distillery company profile, p. 136.]

 Victor Matthews, Ph.D., is a World Master Chef, a Master Bourbon/Whiskey Sommelier, and a master distiller. He is certified as Dining Room Master from the Federation of Dining Room Professionals and an experienced French Quarter bartender. Chef Matthews also is the owner and distiller of Black Bear Distillery in Mountain Falls, Colorado, near Colorado Springs.

National historic Old Crystal Mill on the
Crystal River near Marble, Colorado

PART 2
COMPANY PROFILES & PRODUCTS

WYOMING

Northwest

Northeast

Denver Metro

COLORADO

Southwest

Southeast

NEW MEXICO

Base map © OpenStreetMap.org/copyright

COLORADO: NORTHEAST AREA

Satanka Bay
North Eltuck Cove

Quarry Cave
Elevation 5003
Inlet Bay

Fort Collins

Eaton

Windsor

Spring 44

Loveland

Syntax Spirits
Greeley

Evans

Elkins Distillery
Estes Park

Dancing Pines

Dancing Pines

287

Mead

Spirit Hound Distillers

Longtucky Distilling
Longmont

Black Canyon Distillery

Anvil Distilling

Still Cellars

Geek Spirits

Erie

25

Boulder

Lochbuie

36

Louisville

Brighton

Superior

Broomfield **Mystic Mountain**
Northglenn

Thornton

Westminster

Commerce
City

Arvada

Golden

Wheat Ridge

Idaho Springs

Denver

Aurora

70

Base map © OpenStreetMap.org/copyright

○ Facility and Tasting Room   ● Tasting Room Only
◉ Facility – No Tasting Room

North Fort Collins Detail

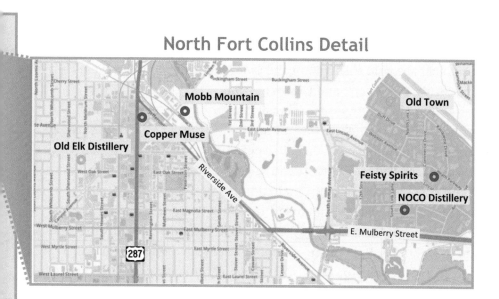

Boulder Detail

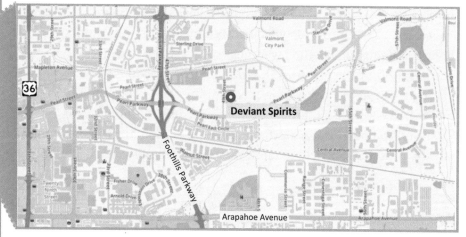

ANVIL DISTILLERY

ANVIL
DISTILLERY

Anvil Distillery spirits include a vodka, an amber rum, a colonial-style gin, and their newest spirit, a light whiskey. Their products are sold throughout the Colorado Front Range, as well as in Florida, New York and Grand Cayman.

Philosophy: Anvil products are hand-crafted spirits, from grain to glass, using the finest ingredients that are locally sourced, organic and non-GMO, whenever possible.

Process & Product Notes: **Grumpy's Vodka** is mashed from non-GMO white corn, with malted millet and malted barley, to bring out the sweetest flavors of the corn. After fermenting the mash for about a week, the vodka is distilled through multiple fractional columns. This process smooths the spirit while retaining a sweet, rich flavor, for a martini or just sipping straight. Grumpy's Vodka was awarded a platinum medal for vodka at the 2015 SIP Awards International Consumer Tasting Competition.

Ironface Gin is created through an additional distillation of their Grumpy's Vodka, in which the "sweet" vapors pass through a collection of nine organic botanicals held in a gin basket, allowing the spirit to pick up all the necessary flavors before being collected. The selection of botanicals was inspired by traditional colonial gin flavors to complement the sweetness of the white corn base. Ironface has a hint of licorice and a tad more citrus than expected, making it perfect as a straight, iced sipping gin.

Fortuity Rum is an amber spirit created using the best cane sugar and the pure water of the Rockies. It is then aged in oak wine barrels, producing a rich, smooth flavor. Originally produced

ADDRESS
117 S. Sunset Street, Suite G1
Longmont, Colorado 80501

OWNER(S)
Peter Grundy, Christa Grundy

CONTACT INFORMATION
720-600-5103
anvildistillery.com
facebook.com/anvildistillerycolorado

TASTING ROOM: YES
TOURS: YES

by Tesouro's, a former Colorado distillery, Anvil now maintains the same recipe, process and aging, continuing the tradition of one of Colorado's finest rums. Fortuity won a gold medal for rum at the 2017 SIP Awards International Consumer Tasting Competition. It also won 1st Place Rum at the 2017 Boulder Crafts Spirits Festival.

FEATURED PRODUCT

Swindler's Light Whiskey is a corn-based spirit with a mash bill similar to bourbon, but distilled at between 161 and 180 proof, creating a sweeter flavor. Head distiller Peter Grundy ages the whiskey for one year in 53-gallon used spiced rum oak barrels from the Caribbean that impart additional flavors and a warm tint to the spirit. These processes qualify Swindler's as a "light whiskey" under TTB requirements.

Swindler's Light Whiskey was awarded a silver medal in the category of "Single Barrel American Whiskey–Up to 10 Years" at the 2017 SIP Awards International Consumer Tasting Competition.

PALE RIDER

- 2 oz Swindler's Light Whiskey
- 1 Bar Spoon Turbinado Sugar
- 1 Fresh Slice of Orange
- 1 Ice Sphere
- 1 oz Club Soda
- 4 dashes Cherry-Hazelnut Bitters

For a twist on a traditional Whiskey Old Fashioned, mix club soda with sugar and whiskey and add bitters. Drop in ice sphere and garnish with orange slice.

Distiller's Tasting Notes: Swindler's Light Whiskey has a smooth, unique sweetness and rich, fragrant body with just a hint of smoke, reminiscent of Highland Scotch without peat. Each batch of Swindler's Light Whiskey is bottled from a single barrel, so each batch tastes slightly different.

BLACK CANYON DISTILLERY

BLACK CANYON spirits include bourbon, corn and infused specialty whiskeys, vodka and liqueurs. Members of Colorado Proud and Made in Colorado, they obtain all ingredients possible from Colorado businesses. Their products are marketed in Colorado, with some specialty whiskeys only available at their tasting room.

Philosophy: For Black Canyon, the term craft spirit means hand crafted to achieve the quality and character they value. They've built the mash tuns, column stills, tasting room bar and tables at their distillery. They also take pride in minimizing their impact on the environment: They recycle cooling water to reduce water consumption, distribute spent mash to local ranchers for their livestock, and salvage stainless steel from old dairy farms. "We tend to look in our own backyard for the raw materials to turn what we imagine into reality," explains co-owner Susan Lesnick.

Process & Product Notes: The bulk of their grains are grown within ten miles of their distillery, and the remainder are high-country grains, which are mixed to yield the desired flavors in their spirits.

Their **Mayhem Creek Pepper Vodka** is infused with fresh jalapeno, habanero, Serrano and Fresno peppers. The use of fresh peppers sets this 80-proof spirit apart from other pepper vodkas for a vibrant Bloody Mary or a spicy mule.

For the 80-proof specialty **Winter Whiskey**, Black Canyon blends their own corn whiskey with organic maple syrup from a family company in Williamsburg, Michigan. Hand-picked Indonesian cinnamon is cracked and steeped in the mixture until whiskey,

ADDRESS
4340 State Highway 66
Mead, CO 80504

OWNER(S)
Fred Lesnick, Susan Lesnick, Nick Sekich,
Dominic Sekich, David Patton, Kathy Patton

CONTACT INFORMATION
720-204-1909
blackcanyondistillery.com
facebook.com/blackcanyondistilling

TASTING ROOM: Yes
TOURS: By appointment

maple sweetness and cinnamon are exactly balanced.

The **Coffee Couloir** liqueur also starts with their corn whiskey, rather than the more commonly used neutral grain spirit. They add vanilla, a cane sugar syrup, plus a cold-press expresso from Paul's Coffee in Louisville, Colorado. It is bottled at 40 proof.

FEATURED PRODUCT

Old Blue Bourbon—named after Charles Goodnight's fabled lead steer for cattle drives out of Texas in the late 1800s—is fermented on the grain for enriched flavor. Head distiller Fred Lesnick uses a lautering process to separate the grain from the wash for a clean liquid that doesn't burn on the heating elements of the 100-gallon electric stills that Fred constructed.

The bourbon ages for a minimum of two years in #3 char, 53-gallon new American white oak barrels and then bottled at 110 proof to capture maximum flavor. Some barrels are being aged three to four years.

OLD SNOWY BLUE

- 1-1/2 oz of Old Blue Bourbon
- 2 oz half-and-half cream
- 1 splash vanilla cream
- 1 splash Coke

In a 12-oz glass, mix ingredients with ice. Similar to a Colorado Bull Dog cocktail that's made with vodka and kahlua instead of bourbon.

Distiller's Tasting Notes: This single barrel, sour mash straight bourbon, has slightly different notes for each barrel. Barrel #1 has a rich amber color and a spicy floral aroma with subtle notes of sweet corn and soft oak. The palate has a lively entry and spicy rich flavor, with caramel and vanilla notes. The finish is clean and sweet with lingering hints of oak and vanilla.

CopperMuse Distillery

COPPERMUSE DISTILLERY owners Jason Hevelone and Heather Trantham, the husband-and-wife team at CopperMuse, were inspired to establish their distillery by the arresting flavor and nuance of a "fateful" Gin & Tonic made from a Colorado craft gin. Distilling and producing carefully hand-crafted spirits suddenly crystalized for them as a perfect way to marry their fermentation skills as practiced brewers and professional engineers with their avid study of the winemaker's use of grape varietals, terroir and oak barrel aging to express their art. It was a life-changing event that propelled them through years of labor to realize a new professional calling as distillers. They now produce a wide range of craft spirits, including bourbon, malt, white and specialty whiskeys, as well as gin, vodka, rum and liqueur, that currently are marketed in Colorado and New Mexico.

Philosophy: For the CopperMuse owners, distilling is a craft and an art. Their convictions: "Hard work and the best ingredients don't mean a thing without inspiration."

Every artist, they believe, needs a muse and their calling is "to find the best inspiration, distill it and share it with the world."

Process & Product Notes: Vertueux Vodka is a classic corn vodka blended to proof with water flowing from fresh Rocky Mountain snow-melt. The water's unique mineral profile is preserved while clarified through a fine-particulate and activated-carbon filtration system, producing an extremely pure, smooth vodka.

Vicieux Black Vodka begins with their Vertueux Vodka and is given its rich, sable color using FDA-certified coloring. It is a crisp,

ADDRESS
244 N. College Avenue, Suite 105
Fort Collins, CO 80524

OWNER(S)
Jason Hevelone and Heather Trantham

CONTACT INFORMATION
970-999-6016
coppermuse.com
facebook.com/thecoppermuse

TASTING ROOM: Yes
TOURS: Yes

bold vodka without the overbearing taste of flavored vodkas.

The CopperMuse **Infusionist Series** offers five vodkas with distinct flavors using only fresh ingredients: cucumber, jalapeno, lavender, bacon and horseradish.

Featured Product

CopperMuse Gold Rum is an award-winning spirit that has received numerous gold medals. The cane-sugar rum has an exceptionally large proportion of molasses in the mash bill to attain its vital flavor intensity. The spirit is aged in sourced used bourbon barrels. The small amount of bourbon soaked within the oak barrels then marries with the rum during the months of aging, bringing out characteristics of butterscotch and caramel. The addition of dark roasted French oak staves adds further complexity. Once fully matured, the now golden rum is fine filtered to remove all particulates and then cut with pure Rocky Mountain spring water for bottling.

Strawberry Fields Martini

Garden fresh strawberries balanced perfectly with balsamic acidity.

- 2 oz Vicieux Black Vodka
- 4 fresh strawberries
- 1/2 oz balsamic vinegar
- 1/2 oz lime juice
- 1/2 oz simple syrup
- 1/2 oz grenadine

Wash and muddle the strawberries in the base of a shaker. Add Vicieux Black Vodka, balsamic vinegar, lime juice, simple syrup and grenadine. Shake over ice and strain into a chilled martini glass.

Distiller's Tasting Notes: The Golden Rum's notes of vanilla, molasses and caramel blend seamlessly with its earthy oaken smoothness. A golden rum worthy of enjoying neat or mixing with just a touch of bitters, sugar and lemon in a rum Old Fashioned.

DANCING PINES DISTILLERY

DANCING PINES Distillery crafts its spirits in small batches with each bottle numbered by batch. Their spirits include bourbon, corn, malt and specialty whiskeys, as well as gin, rum, vodka and liqueur, which are distributed widely in Colorado. They have a tasting room in Breckenridge and in Estes Park, each located in a historic building.

Philosophy: Dancing Pines was inspired and named for the wilderness forests of Colorado. They work to incorporate the freshness of nature in their products by using natural, high-quality ingredients from Colorado sources. They create and flavor their spirits with only whole ingredients—no extracts, no artificial flavorings, no GMOs. "We believe, as stewards of the earth, we each have the responsibility to cherish and preserve it for others."

They put further meaning into their words by actively supporting charitable organizations as well as paying for each of their employees to spend forty hours per year enhancing local wilderness, forest and park areas.

Process & Product Notes: All spirits are distilled and matured in-house, through the combined skills of their master brewer, master distiller and master blender.

The **Dancing Pines Awry** is 100-percent, unblended rye whiskey, aged over three years in their own used bourbon barrels.

DISTILLERY ADDRESS
1029 2nd street
Berthoud, CO 80513

TASTING ROOM ADDRESS
207 Park Lane
Estes Park, Colorado 80517

2ND TASTING ROOM (SEE CO-NW MAP)
201 N. Main Street
Breckenridge, Colorado 80424

OWNER(S)
Jody Thorpe

CONTACT INFORMATION
970-532-1300
dancingpinesdistillery.com
facebook.com/Dancing-Pines-Distillery-301887483095

TASTING ROOM: Yes
TOURS: By appointment

It has received a rating of 90 points from Wine Enthusiast.

Their **Black Walnut Bourbon** starts with their Straight Bourbon and is finished with black walnuts and a touch of blackstrap molasses, placed directly into the Straight Bourbon barrel.

The **Chai Spiced Tea Liqueur** is made with whole, loose leaf tea and spices and sweetened with cane sugar. No corn syrup is used. This liqueur received a rating of 96 points and Top 50 Spirits award in *Wine Enthusiast*, and also double gold at the San Francisco World of Spirits competition.

FEATURED PRODUCT

The award-winning **Dancing Pines Straight Bourbon** has a grain bill of 75% corn, 12.5% rye and 12.5% barley, all locally grown and organic, non-GMO grains. It is aged a minimum of two years in 53-gallon new American oak barrels. The aging process is accelerated by being at elevation with large barometric fluctuations.

CHAI MANHATTAN

A popular twist on a pre-Prohibition cocktail

- 2 oz Dancing Pines Awry
- 1 oz Chai Spiced Tea liqueur
- 2 dashes orange bitters
- 1 cherry

Stir with ice, strain into a chilled martini glass. Serve with a fine cherry.

Distiller's Tasting Notes: The Straight Bourbon nose is sweet maple syrup, turning into vanilla cake with hints of paper and a walk through the forest. The mouth has a rich and velvety texture, followed up with notes of stone fruit and leather, sherry spices and a hint of black pepper. Its finish is long and slightly sweet, with notes of oak.

DEVIANT SPIRITS

DEVIANT SPIRITS makes vodka and gin, which are distributed in Colorado. They have a bourbon scheduled for release in 2018 and also make liqueurs that are served only at their tasting room.

Philosophy: Deviant Spirits was founded in a quest for innovation and readiness to "deviate from the norm" to create a personally rewarding business and to produce the highest quality spirits for their customers.

The company began in a basement where three friends labored to build a superb and unique vodka. They tell a story of dedication where, after twelve solid months of development that required investment of all their collective savings, they emerged with a vodka of such quality that they had to share.

The three friends thus became partners in Deviant Spirits, and they recall this history everyday in their company slogan: "Through passion, art and ingenuity, Deviant Spirits offers the nation's most unique and enjoyable rice-based vodkas, gin and liqueurs."

Process & Product Notes: DV8 Gin is made in small batches from 100-percent, medium-grain calrose rice sourced from California. The spirit is distilled thirteen times and infused with ten botanicals, including cardamom, juniper, coriander, orris root, angelica, casia, cubeb peppers and lavender. The heads and tails cuts are made by hand to ensure the purity of the hearts. The gin is left unfiltered to retain its botanical flavors and create a more full and rich mouthfeel.

DV8 Gin is soft yet complex, with primary scents of lavender and juniper and a flavor profile that is cardamom and orris root

ADDRESS
2480 49th Street, Suite E
Boulder, CO 80301

OWNER(S)
Rawley Gunnels, Johnathan Tilley,
Jeremy Moyers

CONTACT INFORMATION
719-440-4477
deviantspirits.com
facebook.com/deviantspirits

TASTING ROOM: Yes
TOURS: Yes

forward. It is crafted primarily as a sipping gin meant to be enjoyed neat or on the rocks to fully experience the depth of its character. Earthy, simple flavors, such as rose buds, elderflower, shishito leaf or ginger beer, are recommended for any cocktail pairings.

FEATURED PRODUCT

DV8 Vodka is a rice-based spirit. The process begins in a custom-designed bain-marie, double-boiler mash tun. This ancient style of mash tun heats very evenly and avoids scorching the rice and causing off-flavors in the final product. After fermentation is complete, head distiller Jeremy Moyers distills the spirit in a reflux column still, with heads and tails cut by hand. Unlike a traditional pot still, this style of still cycles the fermented rice between vapor and liquid many, many times to achieve extremely high purity in the final product.

THE BERRYOSKA

- 2 oz DV8 Vodka
- 3 oz lemonade
- 2 strawberries
- 3 mint leaves

Muddle strawberries and mint leaves in rocks glass. Add ice. Stir in lemonade and DV8 Vodka.

Distiller's Tasting Notes: DV8 vodka differs from the average vodka experience in its flavor, mouthfeel and nose. Starting with a sweet nose that brings toasted marshmallow to mind, DV8 vodka has a soft introduction to a complex body. The vodka has a full mouthfeel reminiscent of some sakes, full but gentle. The flavor is a well-rounded mix of subtle sweetness with notes of banana and anise, while maintaining a traditional spirit forward flavor and a fresh finish.

ELEVATION 5003 DISTILLERY

ELEVATION 5003 Distillery is a family-owned, grain-to-bottle distillery that grew out of almost two decades of experience in the brewing industry. Their products are distributed in Colorado and include bourbon, corn, malt, rye and white whiskeys, as well as gin, vodka and liqueur.

Philosophy: Founder Loren Matthews tells how her parents told each of their children to pursue careers that they enjoyed, and not look back on life with regret at not taking chances. With fifteen years working in the brewing industry, she decided to try out a home still and immediately fell in love with distilling.

"So, as I shared my passion of brewing and distilling with my friends, the 'starting my own distillery' seed was planted," she recalls. "After a few years, I took the leap of faith and followed my passion for distilling. I don't want to look back on life and regret not doing something I'm passionate about. Cheers to following your dream!"

Process & Product Notes: Narrow Road Vodka, a single malted barley-based vodka, is triple distilled and triple filtered. Narrow Road Vodka has a slightly fruity, estery aroma, with a smooth middle and nutty (almost cocoa) end. Serve neat, on the rocks or in your favorite cocktail.

Lunarshine Corn Whiskey, an unaged, small-batch 100-percent yellow corn whiskey, has an aroma full of spice, with hints

ADDRESS
2601 S. Lemay Avenue. #8
Fort Collins, CO 80525

OWNER(S)
Loren Matthews

CONTACT INFORMATION
970-568-8356
elevation5003.com
facebook.com/elevation5003distillery

TASTING ROOM: Yes
TOURS: By appointment

of toffee and butter pecan. It has a dry, medium-light body with fruit that is silky with tastes of molasses cookie and home-made corn bread. A perfect corn whiskey for sipping or mixing with your favorite cocktail.

Their Caribbean-style **Falernum Liqueur** is distilled with an infusion of all-natural ingredients, including almond, ginger, clove, allspice and lime. This style of liqueur is a longtime staple at resorts and bars in the Caribbean.

Enjoy the liqueur in your Rum Swizzle, Mai Tai, Zombie, Royal Bermuda Yacht Club, Corn n' Oil, or simply serve over ice.

FEATURED PRODUCT

Timber Ridge Gin, an international-style gin distilled in small batches through their column still, has a citrus-forward aroma with orange and lemon peels and a smooth taste from herbs like coriander and cardamom, all of which are recognizable by many imbibers.

The juniper in this gin is sourced locally from juniper bushes around Fort Collins, adding to the special balance of eight different botanicals in the gin.

COLORADO SLING

- 2 oz Lunarshine Corn Whiskey
- 1 oz Falernum Liqueur
- 3/4 oz blackberry shrub
- 1/4 oz lemon juice
- Blackberries
- Ginger beer

Muddle two blackberries in a highball glass, then mix in Lunarshine whiskey, liqueur, lemon juice and blackberry shrub (shrub made with equal parts fruit, sugar and vinegar). Top with ginger beer.

ELKINS DISTILLING CO.

ELKINS
COLORADO WHISKY
ESTES PARK

THE FOUNDERS of Elkins Distilling each came to Estes Park with a searching curiosity about the Rocky Mountains and then were separately but similarly captured by the inspiring locale. A third commonality, however, brought them together as business partners. Each has roots in the South, with a personal and authentic connection to the Southern craft of homemade liquor.

At Elkins Distilling they make corn and white or new-make whiskey, as well as liqueur, which are distributed in Colorado.

Philosophy: Elkins Distilling is dedicated to making the most authentic Colorado whiskey by sourcing ingredients from Colorado whenever possible and using organic ingredients when available. They study, research and experiment with the best ways to mature and blend their products. "Whiskey is our passion," they say, adding: "The view of the Rocky Mountains ain't bad either."

Process & Product Notes: Elkins Corn Whisky, an award-winning, smooth and unaged clear whiskey, grew out of their efforts to craft an authentic Colorado take on a Southern corn whiskey. They use a mash bill of 80% corn, 12% rye and 8% barley—the base formula for all their whiskey products. The equipment for the distillation process includes two stainless pot stills (a 300-gallon stripping still and a 100-gallon finishing or spirit still), five fermenters and two condensers.

Elkins Corn Whisky is a favorite of traditionalists and white lightning enthusiasts, and it makes an interesting full-flavored substitute in vodka, rum and tequila cocktails.

ADDRESS
1825 N. Lake Ave.
Estes Park, Colorado 80517

OWNER(S)
Joe Elkins, McShan Walker,
Nathan Taylor

CONTACT INFORMATION
970-480-1848
elkinswhisky.com
facebook.com/elkinswhisky

TASTING ROOM: Yes
TOURS: By appointment

To make **Colorado Apple Liqueur**, their Corn Whisky is proofed down with organic Colorado apple cider from Palisade. With additions of real cinnamon, Colorado brown sugar and vanilla, they complete their Colorado version of a Southern classic.

While grounded in corn whiskey, they are planning barrel-aged whiskeys from Colorado rye and Colorado malted barley. Recently the Town of Estes Park approved a statute change that allows Elkins to move from a 120-gallon storage capacity to a 1600-gallon capacity. They will use traditional 53-gallon used whiskey and wine barrels plus new oak barrels in a variety of sizes.

FEATURED PRODUCT

Elkins Colorado Whisky begins with their popular Corn Whisky, which then is finished through extensively-tested processes for accelerated mellowing using ultrasonic waves, oxygen and a hydrothermal bath steeped on toasted French and American oak. They also utilize second-use bourbon, Tennessee whiskey and wine barrels.

BUCK AND BLANCO

The first drink Elkins served! A version of the Prohibition-era "Horsefeather."

- 2 oz Elkins Corn Whisky
- 4 oz spicy ginger ale
- 1 dash bitters
- 1 lemon twist

Served on the rocks in an Old Fashioned glass.

Distiller's Tasting Notes: Elkins Colorado Whiskey is a potent but smooth spirit. The palate is sweet and light, mildly fruity and somewhat earthy, with flavors of fresh bread grains and fresh wood.

FEISTY SPIRITS

FEISTY SPIRITS, founded in 2012, makes whiskey—bourbon, corn, malt, rye, wheat, white and specialty-as well as liqueur. Their products are distributed in Colorado.

Philosophy: Feisty Spirits shows its attitude and ethos right up front in their name: a feisty spirit. Founder Jaime Gulden puts it this way: "Feisty people create change. Mahatma Gandhi was Feisty. Nelson Mandela was Feisty. Mother Teresa was Feisty. Martin Luther King was Feisty.

"Being Feisty is about not accepting the world as it is, but instead, choosing your own path and following it. Sometimes it takes you where you think you were going, but many times it doesn't. However, you learn something each time."

Process & Product Notes: Rockit 100% Rye Whiskey is a single-barrel, single-grain organic rye whiskey. The first impression is deep caramel, light notes of spicy rye and a touch of smoke from the barrel. The aroma carries hints of pear, apple and notes of fig. More subtle flavors include dark fruits and brown sugar, and the spicy rye combines with pleasant oak tannin. The smooth finish features a lingering light caramel, with a touch of smoky sweetness.

Rhapsody Blue Corn Bourbon starts with somewhat buttery, almond cream notes, with deep brown sugar and slightly sweet caramel notes. The flavor has a light sweetness from the blue corn which leaves a nice smooth mouthfeel that balances the sweet caramel and moderately-aggressive oak. Finishes with a moderate spice.

ADDRESS
1708 E. Lincoln Avenue, Unit 1
Fort Collins, CO 80524

OWNER(S)
Jamison Gulden, David Monahan

CONTACT INFORMATION
970-444-2386
feistyspirits.com
facebook.com/FeistySpirits

TASTING ROOM: Yes
TOURS: Yes

Their **Maple and Cinnamon Whiskey** is a mellow whiskey infused with real maple syrup and Saigon cinnamon. This light-bodied whiskey has a sweet, maple and tea aroma. The taste begins with light maple flavor, while the cinnamon comes through on the back and lingers. The mouth is rich but not syrupy. Overall the spirit is lightly sweet and easy to drink, with only hints of the mellow whiskey in the background.

FEATURED PRODUCT

With **Better Days Bourbon**, Feisty Spirits presents a single-barrel, four-grain bourbon with spelt and all organic grains. It is aged in 53-gallon, new American oak barrels. To bring in different flavors, they also occasionally finish this single-barrel whiskey in small-batches in used beer, wine, brandy or rum barrels. Each barrel is tasted over time and it is harvested when the flavors match the desired profile.

FEISTY BOURBON JULIUS

- 1 oz Better Days Bourbon
- 1/2 oz Cinnamon Oat Whiskey
- 4 oz orange juice
- 1 oz half & half cream
- 1/2 oz simple syrup
- 3/4 oz egg white
- A few drops vanilla extract
- 1 orange wedge (garnish)

Add all cocktail ingredients to a shaker glass filled with ice. Shake hard and well. Pour into 8 oz glass and garnish with orange wedge. Tip: Egg white in a carton is much easier than using a real egg.

Distiller's Tasting Notes: Better Days Bourbon starts with a light spicy aroma that combines with the big oak, brown sugar and caramel expected from a classic bourbon. Spice and caramel throughout the pallet mix with dark fruits and a strong oak at the finish. The medium dryness of the finish accentuates the oak as well as the light rye subtleties. As a single-barrel spirit, there are unique nuances in aroma and flavor with each barrel

GEEK SPIRITS

GEEK SPIRITS makes rum and bourbon and malt whiskeys. A rye whiskey is scheduled for release by early 2019. They distill, age and bottle all their products at their facility in Boulder. Their products are sold at selected outlets in Colorado and New Mexico.

Philosophy: Geek Spirits was established as an important component of the decision by owners Greg and Sherial Starr to create a better-lived life in Boulder, after decades of high-stress jobs in Silicon Valley. Their rededication to "quality in life" is expressed by their philosophy as distillers: "Geek Spirits uses the finest raw ingredients, science, art and a little bit of magic to produce the best spirits."

Process & Product Notes: **Geek Spirits Silver Rum** is distilled from premium Caribbean molasses in the traditional method to enhance the tropical notes of the spirits. Bottled at 92 proof, it has a full-bodied taste with pineapple and banana notes and toffee nuances.

Geek Spirits Golden Rum is a blend of rum matured in new American oak and used bourbon whiskey casks. Also bottled at 92 proof, it is smooth with tropical fruit flavors and a punch of vanilla. The finish has a taste of caramel.

Geek Spirits award-winning **Spiced Rum** is patiently matured with twelve spices to create a mellow symphony of flavors: vanilla, nutmeg and cinnamon for a rich creamy finish. It is bottled at 92 proof.

ADDRESS
6880 Winchester Circle, Unit D
Boulder, CO 80301

OWNER(S)
Sherial Starr and Greg Starr

CONTACT INFORMATION
303-330-4781
geekspirits.com
facebook.com/GeekSpiritsDistillery

TASTING ROOM: Yes
TOURS: By appointment

Geek Spirits **Formula 37, American Single Malt Whisky** is created from a blend of malted and peat-smoked malted barley. The grain is ground by hand to achieve the ideal grist size for maximum starch conversion. Head distiller Greg Starr employs a two-stage fermentation process to create a high ester mash, which is distilled at approximately 151 proof. Once distilled, the spirit matures in stainless steel before being cut with a local spring water for barreling.

The distillery initially used 53-gallon barrels but moved to 30 gallons for better production flow. Barrels are stored in their 4500 square-foot facility. Although "marginally" temperature-controlled, the storage area experiences temperature swings, which helps with the aging process. Except for these temperature fluctuations, no special processes to speed up the aging are applied. The normally slow extraction and oxidation process is permitted to develop the whiskey's flavors.

S'MORE OLD FASHIONED

- 2 oz Single Malt Whisky
- 3/4 oz graham cracker syrup*
- 3 dashes Angostura bitters
- 1 s'more
- 1 orange slice

In mixing glass, combine Geek Spirits whiskey, syrup and bitters with ice and stir. Garnish with small s'more atop an orange slice, all held with a bamboo cocktail toothpick; pretty easy if you make the s'mores ahead.

*Syrup: 1 cup sugar, 1½ cups water, 4 crushed graham crackers. Stir and heat ingredients. Let cool. Blend and strain.

Distiller's Tasting Notes: Geek Spirits limited release, lightly peated single-malt whiskey is matured in new American oak casks to produce its light amber color with a smoky honey nose. It's a sipping whiskey that opens up with a bit of water to show flavors of clove, vanilla and pineapple. The spirit is bottled at 102 proof to ensure full flavor.

LONGTUCKY SPIRITS

Longtucky Spirits founders, John Abbott Young and Howard K. Wallace, transitioned to craft spirits after working in the craft beer industry as brewers at Avery Brewing and at Upslope Brewing, respectively. The micro-distillery makes whiskey, rum, gin and liqueur. Releases of barrel-aged spirits are scheduled for 2018 (rum) and 2019 (bourbon and rye whiskey). Their products currently are sold at their own cocktail lounge and at retail locations primarily in the Boulder-Longmont area.

Philosophy: Longtucky Spirits focuses on their local Longmont community through their products and as a destination location. They work to celebrate the rich agricultural history of Longmont while creating innovative spirits with ingredients from surrounding farmlands. The expansive cocktail lounge in their renovated facility in downtown Longmont is a venue for live music and provides private meeting space for budding entrepreneurs. It retails their products, serves creative cocktails and conducts educational distillery tours.

Process & Products Notes: All products are double pot-distilled in their personally-built alembic pot-stills. The distinctive, tall pot-still caps provide a clean, full flavor.

Lusca Spiced Rum uses a sour mash—to deepen flavors of sugar beet sugar (75%), from the local Colorado staple crop, and Florida organic molasses (25%)—which is distilled and blended with black cardamom, vanilla, orange, allspice, clove and mace.

ADDRESS
350 Terry Street, Suite 120
Longmont, CO 80501

OWNER(S)
John A. Young, Howard K. Wallace III

CONTACT INFORMATION
720-545-2017
longtuckyspirits.com
facebook.com/longtuckyspirits

TASTING ROOM: Yes
TOURS: Yes

Alpine Dry Gin rejuvenates a traditional style using Colorado ingredients—juniper, spruce tip, sage and lavender—to capture a mountain essence.

Forever Young Malt Whiskey is distilled from a smoked Porter grain base for a new-make spirit tasting of chocolate and roasted malts. It provides a solid backbone to a favorite whiskey cocktail.

FEATURED PRODUCT

Longtucky Fire is a spiced version of their Shine new-make or "moonshine" corn whiskey that head distiller Howard K. Wallace makes with 91% corn and 9% malted barley, both from nearby Colorado sources.

The grains are milled right before mashing for the freshest grain flavors. After double distilling in their pot still, the whiskey is blended with real cinnamon and ginger.

Distiller's Tasting Notes: The moonshine has a clean, full flavor that provides an earthy foundation for the festive spices, with a sweetness from the sugar, but not syrupy sweet.

CINNAMON, SPICE & EVERYTHING NICE

- 2 oz Longtucky Fire
- 3 orange slices
- 1 lemon slice
- Ginger beer
- Ice in shaker

Muddle 2 orange slices and lemon slice. Add to Longtucky Fire and shake with ice. Strain into Collins glass filled with ice. Top with ginger beer and garnish with remaining orange slice.

MOBB MOUNTAIN DISTILLERS

MOBB MOUNTAIN products currently include a rye whiskey and a rye gin. A single-malt whiskey is aging and scheduled for release in 2018. They sell their spirits and cocktails at their newly remodeled tasting room, and they distribute to selected retailers in Colorado.

Philosophy: "Mobb Mountain Distillers is about more than just whiskey." This statement expresses their individual and business commitments to "values of community, adventure, sustainability and quality." Mobb Mountain co-owner and distiller Noah Kroencke explains, "We're driven by a passion for the outdoors and a desire to share those memorable moments with the world. And we see whiskey as the way to bring people together." As part of making fine spirits in a grain-to-glass production facility, they also work to make a perfect gathering place to enjoy them. "You'll be hard pressed," he notes, "to find a day in our tasting room when at least one of the owners isn't there to share a drink with you."

Process & Product Notes: As a grain-to-glass distiller, they mash, ferment, distill and age their products in their own facility. Distillation is performed with a 100-gallon pot still, enabling each batch to be precisely crafted. As a smaller distillery in Northern Colorado, Mobb Mountain explicitly focuses on quality before quantity.

Mobb Gin, a malt gin made with unaged rye mash, is crafted in the style of a traditional Dutch Genever, a precursor to classic dry gin. Unlike London Dry gin, it replaces a neutral vodka-style base with malty 100-percent rye. The gin is distilled three times,

ADDRESS
400 Linden Street
Fort Collins, CO 80524

OWNER(S)
Noah Kroencke, Patrick Moriearty,
Dave Grant, Daniel SansCrainte

CONTACT INFORMATION
970-689-3887
mobbmountain.com
facebook.com/mobbmountaindistillers

TASTING ROOM: Yes
TOURS: Yes

introducing botanicals on the second and third distillation. Spruce tips, coriander and local hops begin the botanical bouquet, with grapefruit peel and juniper added last. The layered botanicals give a mild sweetness from the spruce and an underlying presence of juniper. The body of the spirit is earthy and round from the hops and coriander, while the finish has a slight tartness from the grapefruit.

FEATURED PRODUCT

Their **Rocky Mountain Rye Whiskey** begins with 100-percent malted rye grain. The mash itself is reminiscent of a black tea, and a hybrid American single-malt whiskey yeast gives interest with esters of banana and clove. Head distiller Noah Kroencke double distills the spirit on his pot still (named "Arlene"), bringing a traditional and bold flavor to the whiskey.

Mobb Mountain Rye is aged on a toasted oak, rather than a char, to bring out nut and grain flavors, while preserving the cereal flavor of the rye malt in the finished product. During aging, the spirit is monitored for quality in order to bottle at its peak flavor profile.

Distiller's Tasting Notes: Mobb Mountain Rye Whiskey has forward flavors of nut, smoke, clove, pepper and some floral accents, while the finish brings smooth tones of pecan and mellow oak. A full-bodied spirit, Mobb Rye is best sipped or built into a bold, simple cocktail.

THE MOBB OLD FASHIONED

- 2-1/2 oz Mountain Rye Whiskey
- 1 sugar cube
- 2 splashes Angostura bitters
- 1 Luxardo cherry
- 1 slice lemon peel
- Ice

Thoroughly muddle a sugar cube splashed twice with bitters in a rocks glass. Add ice and the cherry, gently squished. Pour Mountain Rye Whiskey over the ice, stir and garnish with zest of the lemon peel.

NOCO Distillery

NOCO Distillery makes whiskey, gin, rum, vodka and liqueur. They also produce liquors, such as absinthe and blue agave spirits, for limited release or just their tasting room. They distribute products in Colorado, mainly the northern Front Range, and in California, Illinois, Nevada and New York.

Philosophy: NOCO Distillery conducts their business with a strong community orientation. A member of Colorado Proud, they outsource processes where they can to local companies. For example, they contract their wash to local breweries.

Their community focus also involves an ethic to reduce their business' environmental impacts, including recycling or reusing materials from their processes and cutting total energy consumption by almost a third using heat exchangers to preheat succeeding batches. They strive to use organic and non-GMO raw materials when available from their suppliers.

Their small tasting room is built mostly from reclaimed materials and designed to be a splendid meeting place—"A must add to your bucket list when in Fort Collins," they say.

Process & Product Notes: NOCO Brandy/Eau-de-vie is distilled from wine using their smallest fruit stills (13 gallon), then aged in second-use, five-gallon single-malt whiskey barrels. Their brandy also undergoes an additional, proprietary aging method for a more mature and smooth finish.

NOCO Gin is made differently than the traditional approach of most other gin producers. Each botanical is distilled separately.

ADDRESS
328 S. Link Lane #11
Fort Collins, CO 80524

OWNER(S)
Sébastien Gavillet, Leif Jensen

CONTACT INFORMATION
702-234-3602
nocodistillery.com
facebook.com/nocodistillery

TASTING ROOM: Yes
TOURS: No

The separate spirits then are blended selectively and for utmost consistency. This also allows them to produce several types of gins, as well as custom formulations.

NOCO Aged Rum is made from sugar cane and various types of molasses which are fermented and distilled separately in pot and column stills. They mature in five-gallon American oak casks that were used previously to age their whiskeys.

FEATURED PRODUCT

NOCO Blended Whiskey is processed in hand-crafted American-made copper stills. Partner and head distiller Sébastien Gavillet runs the stills slowly to achieve the upmost quality. The blended whiskey matures for six months in five-gallon American oak casks. They follow a proprietary aging procedure developed to mature the spirits faster without compromising on quality.

NOCO ELDERFLOWER COLLINS

- 1-1/2 oz NOCO Brandy
- 1/2 oz elderflower syrup
- 2 oz fresh lemon sour
- 1 rosemary sprig
- Club soda

Shake all with ice except club soda. Strain into a tall glass or wine glass filled with ice and top with club soda.

Distiller's Tasting Notes: The Blended Whiskey has an intense, complex nose with aromas of caramel, apricot, raisin, honey, leather, spices and citrus. The palate is super smooth, with tastes of toffee, ash, nutmeg, dried fruits, tea chest, vanilla and oak. Its smooth finish is long, with notes of orange peel.

OLD ELK DISTILLERY

OLD ELK Distillery currently produces bourbon, a specialty bourbon cream, and gin, with new releases planned for 2019. Their products are distributed in Colorado, California, Kansas, Minnesota, Nebraska, New Hampshire and Virginia.

Philosophy: Old Elk's founders, Curt and Nancy Richardson, position their business as an innovator: "We are passionate about building premium brands and crafting spirits with the goal to elevate the category landscape through innovation."

Process & Product Notes: **Nooku Bourbon Cream** is a true bourbon cream crafted using Old Elk's high-malt bourbon recipe blended with fresh dairy cream. Nooku contains no artificial coloring, added sugar or supplemental spirits. Nooku Bourbon Cream was awarded Gold at the 2017 New York International Spirits Competition.

Dry Town Gin is distilled using ten botanicals: juniper, orris root, orange, lime, angelica root, black pepper, ginger, lemongrass, french verveine and sage. It has a smooth body with distinct herbal, piney and citrus flavors. Dry Town Gin won Double Gold at the 2016 New York International Spirits Competition.

FEATURED PRODUCT

The **Old Elk Blended Straight Bourbon** recipe was formulated by Greg Metze and the Old Elk Distillery team at their R&D facility in Fort Collins, where they currently make their clear spirits. They leveraged partners to produce the bourbon, in order to lay down

ADDRESS
315 W Oak Street, Suite 700
Fort Collins, CO 80521

OWNER(S)
Curt & Nancy Richardson

CONTACT INFORMATION
oldelk.com
facebook.com/oldelkbourbon

TASTING ROOM: No
TOURS: No

barrels in 2014 that would then be properly aged for the bourbon's national launch in 2017.

Old Elk worked with three key partners to ensure quality and consistency of the barrel-aged blended bourbon recipe. Every Old Elk Bourbon barrel is hand-selected by their distilling team, which follows sensory and sampling criteria to ensure the barrels create a consistent blended profile year after year.

The Old Elk recipe includes malted barley, rye and corn. By using four times more malted barley than traditional recipes, the bourbon generates sweet, light components. To enhance flavor, Old Elk employs a slow-cut proofing process, where the barreled bourbon is cut, then left to rest, and repeated over a period of 24 to 48 hours. The extended process allows the flavors to marry between stages, until the desired character is achieved, creating an overall smoother bourbon.

Nooku Julep

- 2 oz Nooku Bourbon Cream
- 1/2 oz white crème de menthe
- 5 dashes Angostura bitters

Combine all ingredients in a cocktail shaker. Add ice and shake vigorously for about 20 seconds. Strain into old fashioned glass filled with ice (preferably crushed). Garnish with a sprig of mint.

Blender's Tasting Notes: Old Elk Blended Straight Bourbon has a robust profile combining its high malt content with a spicy-clove essence from the rye, and the traditional rich bourbon character from the corn. The aroma features sweet vanilla and caramel, clove spice, slight maple and nutty almond. The mouthfeel is smooth and coating with lasting flavor and tastes of maple syrup, almond, raw bran, chocolate, deep wood and coconut.

OLD TOWN DISTILLING CO.

OLD TOWN Distilling is a certified organic distillery, one of only a few in Colorado. They make bourbon, rye and white whiskeys, gin and vodka. Their products are distributed in Colorado.

Philosophy: Old Town Distilling was awarded "Colorado Organic Distillery of the Year" from the New York International Spirits Competition, and Jeremy Kempter, founder and head distiller, describes their philosophy: "Our philosophy is based on being an eco-distillery, sourcing native and heirloom grains from Motherlove Legacy Farm in Johnstown, a ten-mile truck drive from the distillery loading dock; using a high-efficiency filtration system for extracting fluoride and chlorine out of municipal water; recycling the previous batch's cooling water for the next day's mash; recirculating condensing water for distillation; re-purposing used equipment and vessels; and purchasing all packaging supplies (glass, cartons, labels and wax) from within the United States."

Process & Product Notes: Old Town Distilling's **Old Standard Organic Rye Whiskey** was the first organic rye whiskey made in Colorado. It is pot distilled using traditional techniques from 100-percent organic winter rye and matured in second-use bourbon barrels for an average of one year. It received a gold medal at the Micro Liquor Spirit Awards in Beverly Hills, California.

Their **Old Standard Organic Corn Whiskey** is a white (moonshine) whiskey crafted from 80% organic sweet corn, 19% organic winter rye and 1% organic chocolate barley malt from Wisconsin. It is double distilled and aged in stainless steel for several weeks to fully develop. Bottled at 100 proof, it is stout yet smooth.

ADDRESS
513 North Link Lane, Unit E
Fort Collins, CO 80524

OWNER(S)
Jeremy Kempter, Patrick Saul

CONTACT INFORMATION
720-220-6384
oldtowndistilling.com
facebook.com/OldTownDistillingCo

TASTING ROOM: No
TOURS: By appointment

The **Native Nectar Organic Vodka** is distilled six times for great purity from a native Colorado heirloom variety of maize, which gives the naturally sweet spirit tasting notes of dark chocolate and vanilla. Hand bottled at a traditional 80 proof, it has won gold and silver medals at the San Francisco World Spirits Competition.

FEATURED PRODUCT

Old Standard Organic Bourbon Whiskey was the first certified organic bourbon made in Colorado. It has a mash bill of 70% organic sweet corn and 30% organic winter rye. The spirit is aged an average of one year in 15-gallon, new American white oak barrels with No. 4 char. While bottled at a hearty 90 proof, the finished product is free of any harsh alcohol burn.

Distiller's Tasting Notes: With a high-rye mash bill, Old Standard Organic Bourbon features the best of both whiskey families—a sweet and robust corn whiskey character enriched with soft, fruity and floral rye grain flavors. Initially there is remarkable complexity with delicate notes of ripe peach and plum stone fruits and an herbaceous character hinting at anise. These flavors merge with traditional bourbon hallmarks—rich caramel, vanilla, mature oak and smoke—and subtle rye spice qualities, including cinnamon and clove.

MAN O'WAR

- 2 oz Old Standard Organic Bourbon
- 1 oz orange Curaçao
- 1/2 oz sweet vermouth
- 1/2 oz fresh lemon juice
- 1 orange or lemon twist
- 1 brandied cherry

Add first four ingredients to a shaker and fill with cracked ice. Shake and strain into a chilled cocktail glass. Garnish with the orange or lemon twist and brandied cherry on a cocktail pick.

SPIRIT HOUND DISTILLERS

SPIRIT HOUND makes malt whiskey, gin, rum, vodka and liqueur. A four-year rye and a bourbon also are in process. Their products are distributed in Colorado, Kansas and Nebraska.

Philosophy: "The desire to create a completely original Colorado straight malt whisky was the catalyst that brought the Spirit Hound partners together," explains co-owner and distiller Craig Engelhorn.

They also have high regard for traditional whiskey making, while being committed to individuality in crafting their spirits. "We have hand-crafted our own stills, following shapes and dimensions traditional in Scottish whisky production. And our recipes, while based on classic production techniques, are unique."

Process & Product Notes: Spirit Hound Gin features locally-picked Rocky Mountain juniper berries and eight other botanicals, including cinnamon, fennel and citrus zest. They vapor-infuse the spirit with a small botanical basket in the column, ensuring that the flavor is light, clean and easy-drinking.

To help maintain their local supply of juniper berries, Spirit Hound offers customers one free drink for every two cups of juniper berries that the customer brings to the distillery.

Their **Mountain Bum Rum** has half cane sugar and half fancy Caribbean molasses. It is fermented with a traditional rum yeast cultivated in the Caribbean, and then twice pot distilled and aged for one to two years in their own used barrels.

Made in the Italian tradition, **Colorado Red Sambuca** is infused with whole star anise and dried elderberries, which impart a deep

ADDRESS
4196 Ute Hwy
Lyons, CO 80540

OWNER(S)
Craig Engelhorn, Wayne Anderson,
Matthew Rooney, Neil Sullivan

CONTACT INFORMATION
303-823-5696
spirithounds.com
facebook.com/SpiritHoundDistillers

TASTING ROOM: Yes
TOURS: Yes

red color. Bottled at almost 90 proof, the liqueur is sweet, yet potent.

Featured Product

Spirit Hound's single-barrel **Straight Malt Whisky** uses 100-percent malted barley as the base, which is grown, malted and peat-smoked in Alamosa for a completely Colorado malt whiskey. Distilled in their custom, Scottish-style still, it also maintains a fidelity to tradition. The spirit is aged for at least two years in 53-gallon, full-char new American white oak barrels and bottled at 90 proof. The exact duration for each batch is determined by the distillers, based on taste and sensory evaluation. A cask-strength version also is bottled at about 126 proof.

Aviation

A classic, pre-Prohibition era cocktail that is simple and gin-forward.

- 2-1/2 oz Spirit Hound Gin
- 1/2 oz freshly-squeezed lemon juice
- 3/4 oz Bordeaux cherry syrup
- 1 Bordeaux cherry

Chill a martini glass. In a cocktail shaker with ice, add all ingredients and shake for ten seconds. Strain into chilled glasses and garnish with a Bordeaux cherry. For sweeter palates, add 1/4-1/2 oz more cherry syrup.

Distiller's Tasting Notes: All the batches of Straight Malt Whisky share common vanilla and toasted oak characteristics. However, as a single-barrel whiskey, each barrel has distinct characteristics. Current offerings may be sampled at the tasting room. Tasting notes for each barrel are listed on their website, where you'll see that the nose, as in one example, varies among barrels from earthy and peaty, to sweet herbal, to mild oak, to big vanilla, with comparable nuances across the full sensory profile.

SPRING 44 DISTILLING

SPRING44 MAKES vodka, three gins and a single malt whiskey using only artesian mineral water from their private spring in the northern Colorado Rocky Mountains. They distribute products in Colorado and five other states.

Philosophy: "The proof is in the water," says co-owner Jeff Lindauer about the role of this uniquely sourced ingredient. Spring44 is inspired by the natural spring tucked away on remote land his father purchased nearly fifty years ago in Colorado's Buckhorn Canyon on East White Pine Mountain. The spring is surrounded by 160,000 acres of National Forest and accessible only by navigating an 11-mile dirt road, culminating with a 2.5-mile jeep trail climbing 2,000 feet of elevation.

The pristine environment and pure spring water "set the standard for our products made with this water and our core values of quality, sustainability, authenticity and transparency."

Products & Process Notes: Spring44's 80-proof **Vodka** is made from USA-grown, gluten-free and GMO-free corn. This product was awarded five stars in Paul Pacult's *Spirit Journal* and named one of only two domestic vodkas in his top-ranked 120 best spirits in the world.

Head distiller Jeff McPhie describes their **Honey Vodka** as carrying aromas of lavender and fresh honey "straight from the honeycomb," with hints of vanilla and toasted nuts, and a palate of light honey sweetness up front, plus floral notes and hints of lavender. Mid-palate is creamy with warm vanilla and rich honey and the finish is long with notes of toasted nuts.

ADDRESS
505 W. 66th Street
Loveland, Colorado 80538

OWNER(S)
Jeff Lindauer, Jeff McPhie, Robin Marisco

CONTACT INFORMATION
970-414-0744
spring44.com
facebook.com/Spring44

TASTING ROOM: No
TOURS: No

Old Tom Gin is barrel-aged and produced in a classic manner that dates back to the 18th century. Botanicals include juniper, toasted coriander, orris root, galangal root, fresh grapefruit peel, fresh rosemary and lemongrass.

* * * * *

For maturation and finishing, Spring44 uses new American oak charred, new American oak toasted, and second-use bourbon barrels, in 53-, 60- and 30-gallon sizes.

FEATURED PRODUCT

Spring44 **Mountain Gin** is made from USA grown corn (gluten-free and GMO-free) in two separate distillations. The botanicals include juniper, coriander, orange peel, orris root, kaffir lime leaf, peppermint and basil. At 88 proof, it's bold enough to hold up in a cocktail and floral enough to drink neat or on the rocks.

GARDEN PARTY

- 1-1/2 oz Mountain Gin
- 1/2 oz fresh lime juice
- 3 cucumber wheel slices
- 6 mint leaves, 1 for garnish
- 1/4 oz light agave
- 3 oz tonic

Muddle together mint, two cucumber wheels, lime juice, and agave. Add gin and ice, then shake. Pour tonic into a cocktail glass with one large ice cube. Slowly double strain shaken cocktail over tonic. Garnish with remaining cucumber wheel and mint leaf for a fresh, bright cocktail.

Distiller's Tasting Notes: **Mountain Gin's** aroma carries crisp notes of pine and citrus, with subtle hints of malt, chocolate and earth after rainfall. This is a delightfully dry gin with juniper on the front palate, while the mid-palate showcases coriander and ginger with hints of lime and orange zest. The finish is dry and refreshingly bold with distinct notes of mint.

STILL CELLARS

STILL CELLARS is a certified organic distillery developed as a community gathering place featuring artwork, live performance and artisanal spirits. They make whiskey, vodka, a line of apple brandies, and experimental batches of various spirits. Their products are sold at their tasting room and selected outlets in the Colorado Front Range.

Philosophy: Still Cellars was established to make certified organic distilled spirits and also as a creative arts community center. Their Arthouse acts as the distillery's tasting room and as a venue for local artists to exhibit and perform for the community.

Process & Product Notes: Still Cellars hand-crafts its products from scratch using traditional methods and strict standards. They use whole food ingredients, do not chill filter, and only gently filter the spirits to retain rich ingredient character characteristics. Some amount of sediment or cloudiness, especially in the apple spirits, normally is expected to accompany the enriched flavors.

Apple Straightup is an unoaked brandy, or eau de vie, made with organic apples from the Colorado western slope. Still Cellars ferments and distills approximately twenty pounds of apples per bottle. The spirit then is infused with fresh apples for enriched flavor and sweetness. The final brandy has delicate layers of sweetness, with hints of apple-peel bitterness and honeysuckle. A fine sipping brandy, it also swaps well for traditional brandies, whiskey and sometimes even vodka in many classic recipes.

Still Cellars **Apple Ginger** brandy begins with their Apple Straightup, which they infuse with dried ginger root, capturing

ADDRESS
1115 Colorado Avenue, Suite C
Longmont, CO 80501

OWNER(S)
Jason R. Houston, Sadye Rose W.

CONTACT INFORMATION
720-204-6064
stillcellars.com
facebook.com/StillCellars

TASTING ROOM: Yes
TOURS: By appointment

the spicy warmth of the ginger and further balancing the apple's floral sweetness. Apple Ginger retains the ginger's medicinal properties, offering ginger lovers a fine sipping brandy. It pairs well with citrus, fruits, floral and savory herbs, and peppery spices.

Apple Cinnamon brandy again starts with Apple Straightup and then is infused with real cinnamon to produce a smooth and warming sipping brandy that balances sweetness with the bold flavor of cinnamon. It mixes well with cream or milk, cacao, orange and nuts.

FEATURED PRODUCT

Still Cellars presents their **Whiskey Barley** as Colorado's first certified-organic whiskey. Inspired by the character and craft of Old World Scotch, their Whiskey Barley uses a single-malt, 100-percent barley mash that is open-air fermented. Head distiller Jason Houston employs a pot still to manually distill the spirit and then matures the whiskey for two to three years in 25-gallon, new American white oak barrels, lightly toasted.

LADY BEE LAVENDER

- 1-1/2 oz Still Cellars Vodka
- 1/2 oz lavender bitters*
- 1-1/2 oz honey water
- 1 oz coconut water
- 1 tsp fresh squeezed lime juice
- 1 lavender sprig and flowers

Mix over ice: vodka, honey water (1 tsp honey/1 oz water), coconut water, lime juice, lavender bitters. (*Soak 1 oz lavender flowers/750 ml vodka for 7-10 days; or try lavender tincture. Avoid sweetened or flavor lavender products). Shake vigorously and strain into rocks glass. Garnish with lavender flowers and sprig.

Distiller's Tasting Notes: Whiskey Barley has a core tasting profile of bold caramel nose, earthy body and a rich finish, with soft oak and citrus overtones. It is bottled, however, as an unblended single-barrel product, so each barrel yields a batch that has distinctive flavor and aroma profiles.

SYNTAX SPIRITS

SYNTAX SPIRITS makes bourbon, gin, rum and vodka. They plan to release specialty bourbon and rum, both finished in wine barrels, sometime in 2018. The distillery also is moving to the landmark Greeley Grain Elevator Building in summer 2018. Their products are distributed in Colorado, Wyoming and Oklahoma.

Philosophy: Syntax Spirits practices a thoroughly handmade, small-batch approach to distilling, using local ingredients. The distillery was engineered and built by owner and head distiller Heather Bean. All their spirits are made with raw ingredients. They also use sustainable production practices, such as minimizing water use, recycling bottles and packaging, and returning spent grain to local farmers.

Process & Product Notes: **Syntax Crystal Vodka** is made from local wheat and Poudre River mountain water. It is distilled repeatedly in their handmade column still and polished by carbon filtering that makes it smooth enough for sipping, with hints of sweet cereal and citrus flavors. It has won gold medals from the Beverage Tasting Institute and the Microliquor Internatioanl Spirits Awards.

Syntax Heavy Rum, made from Florida dark molasses and aged in bourbon barrels, is smooth and dark, with just a hint of molasses added back. It has flavors of anise, malt and caramel. Think Hot Buttered Rum or Midnight Caipirinha.

Syntax Rose Gin is floral with a blend of eleven herbs and spices, including rose petals, sweet orange peel and lavender

ADDRESS
625 3rd Street, Unit C
Greeley, CO 80631

NEW ADDRESS (SUMMER 2018)
700 6th Street
Greeley, CO 80631

OWNER(S)
Heather Bean, Jeff Copeland

CONTACT INFORMATION
970-352-5466
syntaxspirits.com
facebook.com/syntaxspirits

TASTING ROOM: Yes
TOURS: Yes

flowers. It begins with the Crystal Vodka, which then is distilled with herbs both in the still and in a vapor basket in the still column.

FEATURED PRODUCT

Syntax Straight Bourbon Whiskey is made from local corn, wheat and barley processed with their handmade column stills and proprietary control system. The white spirit must be smooth and flavorful enough to sip as a white whiskey to be accepted for barreling.

Each batch is aged at least two years in 53-gallon new American oak whiskey barrels for a rich bourbon flavor and complex character. Syntax makes some seasonal releases of the bourbon that has been further finished in wine barrels or on other wood. The whiskey is bottled at 95 proof.

Distiller's Tasting Notes. The Straight Bourbon Whiskey is light amber color, with aromas of caramelized nuts, apricot granola, waxy honeycomb and candy corn. Medium-to-full bodied, it is fruity, yet dry. The warm and zesty finish has tastes of peppery spice, dried fruit, dusty grain and mineral.

The Beverage Tasting Institute rated it very highly among craft whiskeys and described it as "A brashly flavorful young bourbon that will add fruit character to whiskey cocktails; try in an old fashioned." The bourbon won two gold medals at both the 2015 and 2017 Wizards of Whisky awards in the United Kingdom.

HARVEST WHISKEY SOUR

- 1 shot Syntax Straight Bourbon
- 1 shot apple cider or apple juice
- 1/2 shot real maple syrup
- 1/2 shot simple syrup
- Juice of one lemon
- A few splashes of Angostura and/or orange bitters (to taste)

Shake and serve over ice in an Old Fashioned glass. Option: Rim the serving glass with vanilla sugar.

COLORADO: DENVER METRO AREA

Mad Rabbit
Whistling Hare
Northglenn
Thornton
Federal Heights
Westminster
Leyden
Arvada
Commerce City
Wheat Ridge
Golden Moon
Golden
Colorado Vodka Co.
Mile High Spirits
Rising Sun
Denver
Stranahan's
Laws Whiskey House
Bear Creek
Devil's Head
Sheridan
Englewood
Rocker Spirits
Greenwood Village
Littleton

E Street
F Street
G Street
West 6th Avenue
Golden Moon
Golden
Local Distilling
State 38
Rooney Road
Commerce Court
Corporate Circle

◉ Facility and Tasting Room   ◉ Facility – No Tasting Room
◉ Tasting Room Only

Leopold Brothers

Aurora

83

285

83

Downslope Distilling

88

Branch and Barrel

Centennial

Bear Creek Distillery

BEAR CREEK
· Distillery ·

BEAR CREEK Distillery spirits include rye, wheat and white whiskeys, bourbon and multiple varieties of rum and vodka. These are available at their cocktail bar and at retailers throughout Colorado and in Wyoming.

Philosophy: Co-owner Jay Johnson explains that at Bear Creek, "We have four pillars of excellence: quality people, quality ingredients, quality machinery and quality spirits." They strive for complete transparency, with all their spirits produced grain-to-bottle at their Denver facility and distilled with their state-of-the-art, German-built Kothe still.

Process and Products Notes: Bear Creek prides itself on using local ingredients, often organic, for their spirits, as well as local ingredients and products at their cocktail bar, which Jay happily notes has been heralded as one of the top Colorado cocktail destinations.

Their **Rye Whiskey** is a medium-bold, 100-percent rye with a sweet cherry and fig finish, having elements of leather and tobacco. The whiskey is aged in 30-gallon new North American oak barrels for approximately two years.

Among their rums, the **Spiced Rum** is a holiday-style spirit, infused with whole spice. It's not overly sweet, with flavors of orange peel, vanilla bean, black pepper, ginger, cinnamon, allspice and nutmeg—all combined to make Christmas in a glass.

Bear Creek's distinctive, 100-percent **Rye Vodka** is a whiskey drinker's vodka, with its own flavor and weight. Jay

ADDRESS
1879 S. Acoma Street
Denver, Colorado 80223

OWNER(S)
Jay Johnson, Jeffrey Dickinson,
Dbo Baker

CONTACT INFORMATION
303-955-4638
bearcreekdistillery.com
facebook.com/BearCreekDistillery

TASTING ROOM: YES
TOURS: By appointment

notes that this vodka is the most consistently-awarded spirit in their lineup.

FEATURED PRODUCT

Bear Creek distills its **Straight Bourbon Whiskey** from a mash bill of 75% organic corn, 15% organic rye and 10% malted barley. They mature the bourbon in 53-gallon, new American white oak barrels in their nonclimate-controlled rackhouse, exposing the spirit to changing temperature and humidity for a robust yet smooth whiskey.

The first batch available to the public is a blend from three-year-old and two-year-old barrels. They are planning single-barrel and cask-strength offerings in the future.

RED PANDA BEAR

A savory, bright vodka cocktail. Plays on notes of sweet and savory. Red bell pepper is the star here.

- 2 oz Bear Creek Rye Vodka
- 1 oz fresh red bell pepper juice
- 1 oz honey syrup
- 1/2 oz fresh lemon juice
- 3 leaves of basil
- Ice

Add all ingredients to a pint glass. Add ice and shake vigorously. Strain into cocktail glass filled with ice.

Distiller's Tasting Notes: The Straight Bourbon Whiskey is distilled one batch at a time at the Denver distillery and then patiently matured in new American white oak barrels. When deemed appropriate, barrels are hand selected to become a single-barrel release or blended to create a unique batch of smooth-finishing, Colorado-style bourbon with notes of tropical fruit and cocoa.

BRANCH & BARREL
BY BROKEN ARROW SPIRITS

BRANCH & BARREL

BRANCH & Barrel products are inspired by a quest to reclaim the quality and premier role of whiskeys at the time of America's founding, when distinctive spirits were made in small batches by individuals perfecting their craft. They currently distill whiskey in three expressions: white oak, red oak and plum. Distributed in Colorado, the three expressions are produced in small batches and each is available only during specific time periods.

Philosophy: The three partners in Broken Arrow Spirits are committed to distilling whiskey using hand-selected local ingredients and the traditional methods of individual craftmanship. They dedicate their products to whiskey's heritage: "We're raising a glass to all that whiskey was and should be again."

They describe this historical role of whiskey: "Our founding fathers drank whiskey. It was even used as currency and to pay off debts. It was so popular, when the government tried to tax it in 1791, ex-Revolutionary War soldiers rebelled and almost broke our new union apart. Whiskey marched on both sides of the Civil War. And it gave cowboys something to look forward to at the end of the trail."

The three partners also undertake their business in service to the community, working with local suppliers but also understanding their whiskey as an expression of friendship—like the Native American peace offering of the "broken arrow." With a 20-year bond as friends themselves, the partners "came together to bring joy and friendship to the whiskey."

ADDRESS
15353 E Hinsdale Circle, Suite C
Centennial, Colorado 80112

OWNER(S)
Ryan Morgan, Tom Sielaff,
Scott Freund

CONTACT INFORMATION
720-663-0468
branchandbarrelwhiskey.com
facebook.com/brokenarrowspirits

TASTING ROOM: YES
TOURS: By appointment

Process & Product Notes: The commitment to traditional, hand-crafted spirits has meant constructing their own fractionating still and recycling machinery from as far back as the 1920s. Corn and barley is supplied from neighboring farms, and wood chips from their backyard trees flavor some of their whiskeys. Spring water from Eldorado Springs is used for all their products. Spirits are aged and finished in barrel sizes of 5, 30 and 53 gallons, depending on the product.

FEATURED PRODUCT

The **Branch & Barrel White Oak Whiskey** is a bourbon processed from local corn and barley. The fractionating still produces 97 percent alcohol content, which is then triple distilled for purity and a more palatable, higher quality and more flavorful whiskey. Head distiller Rick Warren ages the whiskey in 53-gallon, new American white oak barrels.

Distiller's Tasting Notes: The White Oak Whiskey is a robust bourbon, wide and oaky, with sweet caramel and malt flavors.

CO FASHIONED

- 1-1/2 oz Branch & Barrel White Oak Whiskey
- 1/2 oz Amaro
- 2 dashes black walnut bitters
- 2 cubes brown sugar
- 1 orange peel (flamed)

Combine ingredients (except orange peel) in a mixing glass. Stir, then add ice and stir again. Filter ice and pour liquid into a tumbler with one large ice cube. Shave 1" x 2" piece of orange peel. Squeeze peel over glass while lighting a flame beneath the peel. Drop peel in drink. Enjoy.

COLORADO VODKA COMPANY

COLORADO VODKA Company is a local and family-run company dedicated to producing a top-quality vodka for Colorado's active lifestyle. They strive to make their product easily available in Colorado, whether you need to pick up a bottle, say, for your rafting trip or prefer it in your Moscow Mule when hanging with friends at your favorite sports bar. Most bartenders will tell you that there is no other spirit that mixes as well, in so many drinks, as vodka. Their website lists more than 100 retail stores and more than 165 bars and restaurants in Colorado, many in the Denver metro area, that carry their product.

Philosophy: The founders envisioned and built their company with a strong sense of commitment and loyalty to their community and the larger state of Colorado. During much earlier years, when they worked helping to develop the LoDo neighborhood of downtown Denver, they frequently talked about starting their own brand with the state flag on the front of the bottle, a local spirit with a downtown location and identity, working alongside other local and family-run restaurants and companies. They see their success—and also their reward—in commitment to customer service and their community: "We are proud of being from Colorado and being able to have fun doing something we are passionate about—making a top-quality vodka for friends to enjoy!"

Process & Product Notes: Colorado Vodka followed an extensive process of research, blind tastings and consultations with

ADDRESS
2701 Lawrence Street, Suite 20
Denver, Colorado 80205

OWNER(S)
Aaron Steinke

CONTACT INFORMATION
303-667-7491
covodkaco.com
facebook.com/colorado.vodkaco

TASTING ROOM: No
TOURS: No

expert sommeliers, mixologists and a partner distillery to formulate a proprietary recipe having their ideal blend of corn and wheat and sugar. Colorado Vodka works with Mile High Spirits Distillery for production and bottling.

ROCKY MOUNTAIN MULE

A spin on the traditional Moscow Mule without ginger beer! Instead, use CVC Vodka, ginger syrup and Velvet Falernum (Barbados simple syrup) with fresh lime and soda. Fresh and delicious!

- 1-1/2 oz CVC Vodka
- 3/4 oz Bougie Ginger Syrup
- 1/4 oz Velvet Falernum
- 3/4 oz fresh lime juice
- Fresh lime
- Club soda
- Ice

Build over ice—preferably in a traditional copper mule mug. Fill with soda and garnish with a fresh lime.

FEATURED PRODUCT

CVC Vodka is a proprietary blend of corn and wheat (still gluten free) distilled six times in a column still to ensure a clean texture and mouthfeel. This mashbill makes a smooth and lighter vodka than often is produced from potatoes, which can be much heavier in texture, or from fruits that can be tart. It is proofed for bottling with Colorado's Rocky Mountain water.

Blender's Tasting Notes: The vodka is slight and crisp with a traditional nose that leads to a soft mid-palate sweetness and very smooth finish. CVC Vodka's smoothness can be enjoyed just poured over ice. Its blending ability makes for excellent cocktails, and the sweet mid-palate excels in such cocktails as a Bloody Mary, Screwdriver or Martini.

DEVIL'S HEAD DISTILLERY

D EVIL'S HEAD Distillery takes its name from Devil's Head Mountain southwest of Denver. To be established at their Englewood site, Devil's Head had to convince city council, through a yearlong campaign, to revise a decades-old law prohibiting distilleries within the city. They succeeded and now distribute their vodka, gin and aquavit in Colorado, primarily along the Front Range from Denver to Castle Rock.

Philosophy: Founder and distiller Ryan White was inspired by aromatic juniper along the trails on Devil's Head Mountain to build a small-batch distillery for high-quality Colorado native gin, from grain to bottle, with none of the process being outsourced. They mash, ferment, distill and bottle all their products at their Englewood distillery, holding firmly to an ethos to maintain high standards of quality.

Process & Product Notes: Devil's Head uses 100-percent barley for all their spirits. They distill in their custom, American-made Vendome still. The most aromatic and flavorful botanicals are sourced from all over the world and vapor infused into their gin and aquavit during distillation.

Devil's Head Aquavit is a modern take on this Scandinavian staple otherwise known as "Water of Life." Aquavit is produced similarly to gin, but with caraway providing the predominant botanical flavor instead of juniper. Devil's Head Aquavit maintains the caraway tradition while joining it with anise, celery, dill and other hand-crushed aromatic botanicals for a result that is truly unique and well balanced.

ADDRESS
3296 South Acoma Street
Englewood, Colorado 80110

OWNER(S)
Ryan White

CONTACT INFORMATION
720-668-8770
devilsheaddistillery.com
facebook.com/DevilsHeadDistillery

TASTING ROOM: YES
TOURS: By appointment

In **Devil's Head Gin**, the distillery uses seven aromatic botanicals from around the world, hand crushed to expose the fragrant essential oils, and then vapor infused in distilling the spirit. More of an American gin, it is complex yet well balanced, retaining the traditional juniper base with the addition of subtle floral notes.

Devil's Head Vodka is distilled from a mash of 100-percent malted barley and then charcoal filtered for a smooth and refined flavor, while maintaining a subtle hint of sweetness. No added sugar, flavorings or chemicals.

FEATURED PRODUCT

The first batch of **Oak Barrel Reserve Aquavit** was released in late 2017 after aging for eighteen months in new American white oak barrels with a #3 char. Starting with their Devil's Head Aquavit, the aging further enhances and balances the spirit, while adding a rich oak character to its already complex flavor profile.

NOTES OF A DIRTY OLD MAN

The complexity, aroma and herbal qualities of barrel-aged aquavit in a traditional Old Fashioned recipe.

- 2 oz Oak Barrel Reserve Aquavit
- 1/4 oz honey simple syrup
- 3 to 5 dashes aromatic or orange bitters
- 1 large ice sphere
- Grapefruit or orange peel

Fill short glass with ice and add aquavit, honey syrup and bitters. Rim glass with grapefruit or orange peel and garnish with same.

Distiller's Tasting Notes: Devil's Head Aquavit has the spirit's traditional caraway flavor while adding a number of additional botanicals including anise, celery, dill, fennel and others. Barrel aging further enriches the spirit with flavors of oak. The bold, savory and earthy flavor is versatile for traditional cocktails like a Bloody Mary or Old Fashioned, as well as modern craft cocktails.

DOWNSLOPE DISTILLING

DOWNSLOPE DISTILLING

D OWNSLOPE DISTILLING is among the oldest distilleries in Colorado. It currently distributes ten products, including whiskey, gin, rum and vodka, in Colorado and selected products in California. They also make limited-release whiskeys and specialty products that are available only at their tasting room.

Philosophy: Downslope Distilling began with the notion that a dedicated team could produce distinctive, interesting and complex spirits successfully on a small scale. In 2009, less than a year later, Bureau of Alcohol and Tobacco Tax and Trade issued Distilled Spirits Plant Permit number 16 (in Colorado) to the company.

They are proud to have been a pioneer in craft distilling in Colorado and continue to ferment and distill all their spirits in house with their custom-designed copper pot still. "Our passion for the craft prevents us from cutting corners," founder Mitch Abate explains. "We start with raw ingredients, taking them all the way to the finished bottled product. The pride we take in that finished product creates even more drive to make the next batch even better."

Process & Product Notes: All Downslope whiskeys are double distilled with their copper pot still. Their different whiskeys are aged in a variety of barrels, including wine, cognac and new bourbon casks.

Downslope's **Double Diamond Rye Whiskey** is made from 100-percent American rye and aged in a new single bourbon cask for a minimum of two years.

ADDRESS
6770 South Dawson Circle, Suite 400
Centennial, Colorado 80112

OWNER(S)
Chap Nelson, Mitchell T. Abate

CONTACT INFORMATION
303-693-4300
downslopedistilling.com
facebook.com/downslopedistilling

TASTING ROOM: YES
TOURS: Yes

Their **Double Diamond Malt Whiskey** is made from 95% Maris Otter malt and 5% peated malt. It is aged for a minimum of three years in a new bourbon cask and finished in a sherry cask.

Double Diamond Agave Spirits Reposado is made from 100-percent Blue Weber agave that has been pitted, roasted and juiced in the traditional tequila fashion. The juice is fermented in house and double-distilled in their custom pot still. The spirit then is aged in Downslope's own used whiskey casks for a minimum of six months.

FEATURED PRODUCT

Downslope distills its **Double Diamond Whiskey** using 65% floor malted Maris Otter barley from England, selected for its cask aging potential, plus a generous portion (35%) of American rye from Iowa and a small amount of peated barley.

Mitch Abate, also head distiller, utilizes a proprietary yeast strain developed in Scotland, distilling the whiskey in their custom double diamond pot still for maximum flavor development.

The whiskey is aged in red wine casks and finished in small new charred American oak casks for at least two years. During this time it develops a deep ruddy hue and enriched character. Downslope proudly presents this whiskey as a true American craft spirit, "imitating nothing and built layer upon layer according to our inspiration."

DOUBLE DIAMOND HOT DOG

- 2 oz Downslope Pepper Vodka
- 10 oz pink grapefruit juice

Serve this spicy and sour cocktail over ice.

GOLDEN MOON DISTILLERY

logo text

GOLDEN MOON Distillery produces nineteen spirits, including bourbon, malt and rye whiskeys, gin, liqueur, brandy and bitters. Colorado and Wyoming are among the fourteen states where their products are distributed.

Philosophy: Golden Moon Distillery was founded in 2008 specifically to produce premium hand-crafted herbal liquors and liqueurs using the best available herbs, spices and botanicals, with the same type of methods utilized by artisan distillers in the mid-to-late 1800s. The heart of Golden Moon recipes and distilling practices, explains co-founder and head distiller Stephen Gould, is his collection of hundreds of rare books on distillation and related products and processes, most dating from the 1700s to early 1900s.

Golden Moon uses only natural ingredients and sources from local producers whenever possible. They often bottle at higher proof for richer flavor and with less sugar, so that their spirits make a better cocktail and put control of sweetness in the bartender's hands. They use recyclable packaging, and solid waste from distilling processes are used for compost and feed by local farmers and gardeners.

Process & Product Notes: Golden Moon has four antique stills from the beginning to middle of the 1900s. A major expansion now underway will add five more antique stills, two large new whiskey stills and four large multi-purpose stills.

After Gould sampled a late 1800s medicinal gin and experimented with historical gin recipes, he created **Golden Moon Gin** as

DISTILLERY ADDRESS
412 Violet Street
Golden, Colorado 80401

TASTING ROOM ADDRESS
1111 Miner's Alley
Golden, Colorado 80401

OWNER(S)
Stephen Gould

CONTACT INFORMATION
303-993-7174
goldenmoondistillery.com
facebook.com/GoldenMoonDistillery

TASTING ROOM: Yes
TOURS: Yes

a distinctive spirit, with a highly floral aroma, refined flavors and a slight sweetness. Golden Moon presents their **Creme de Violette** as one of the few American-produced violet spirits on the market. It is bottled at higher proof with less sugar for a cleaner, fresher taste in a classic cocktail or enjoyed by itself.

Golden Moon **Amer dit Picon** recreates the original Amer Picon recipe that was discontinued in the late 1800s. Bottled like the original at 78 proof, it is an essential ingredient for an authentic Brooklyn Cocktail, Liberal Cocktail, The Brittany and the Picon Punch.

FEATURED PRODUCT

Golden Moon Colorado Single Malt is made in house from 100-percent two-row barley, from Colorado and surrounding states, and malted in Colorado. Mashing is similar but not identical to a Scottish "three-water" process. They use an atypical yeast and the whiskey is double distilled in a copper pot-still. The spirit is aged first in new American and Hungarian oak casks and then finished in used port and whiskey casks. Bottled at 92 proof, Colorado Single Malt is a smooth and approachable whiskey with nice complexity.

Golden Moon Colorado Single Malt was awarded a Double-Gold Medal at the 2016 San Francisco World Spirits Competition.

THE GOLDEN EAGLE

A frothy, tasty, lemony cocktail that brings smiles.

- 1-1/2 oz Golden Moon Gin
- 3/4 oz Golden Moon Creme de Violette
- 3/4 oz lemon juice
- Angostura bitters

- 1/2 oz rich simple syrup (2 parts sugar, 1 part water)
- 1 egg white
- 1 lemon peel

Shake and strain into a cocktail glass or cup. Angostura bitters design on top. Twist lemon peel over cocktail and discard.

LAWS WHISKEY HOUSE

LAWS WHISKEY House produces only whiskey. These include bourbon, corn, malt, rye, wheat and specialty whiskeys. Their products are widely distributed in Colorado and are also sold in Arkansas, Illinois, New York, Tennessee, Texas and Washington.

Philosophy: For their products, Laws has a firm standard: "Craft over commodity. Quality over quantity. Whiskey above all." To that they add a fourth—"There are no shortcuts." In their business practices, they are committed to transparency and honesty to maintain the trust of their customers.

Process & Product Notes: To achieve their goals for quality, Laws conducts all production steps in house. They use Colorado corn and grain, and employ traditional open-air fermentation to achieve balance and character in the whiskey. They also note that barrel aging of whiskey in Colorado, with the large temperature and pressure fluctuations of the high-plains and mountain climate, accelerates maturation compared with distilleries at low elevation.

A.D. Laws Secale Straight Rye is one of their most popular whiskeys. Made with 100-percent Colorado grains (95% rye and 5% barley) and bottled at 100 proof, this sour-mash whiskey packs a punch. Aged no less than three years, rich flavors and layered complexity refine its characteristic regional terroir.

A.D. Laws Triticum Straight Wheat Whiskey is their homage to wheat, the "Grain of Civilization." Mashed, fermented and distilled to accentuate the welcoming character of its high-mountain, Colorado-grown wheat, Triticum is smooth and approachable with fruit, caramel and baking spice notes.

ADDRESS
1420 S Acoma St
Denver, Colorado 80223

OWNER(S)
Alan D. Laws

CONTACT INFORMATION
720-570-1420
lawswhiskeyhouse.com
facebook.com/lawswhiskey

TASTING ROOM: Yes
TOURS: Yes

A.D. Laws Hordeum Straight Malt Whiskey is made with Hordeum—wild barley grass—one of the world's ancestral grains. With a mash of 99-percent barley plus a bit of rye, the locally-roasted artisan malts lend a nutty flavor, while hints of stewed fruit complement its sweet malt backbone. This grain forward, single-malt whiskey, bottled at 85 proof, showcases the native terroir of Colorado.

FEATURED PRODUCT

A.D. Laws Four Grain Straight Bourbon is the company's distinctive flagship whiskey. The sour-mash whiskey is crafted from all four of the "American mother grains": corn (60%), wheat (20%), barley (10%) and rye (10%). All are sourced from Colorado and processed with pure spring water from Eldorado, Colorado.

To manage the difficult and uncommon production of a four-grain whiskey, owner and head distiller Alan Laws uses a stepped cooking procedure, where each grain variety requires a different cooking temperature to maximize its flavor and character. The grain requiring the most heat is milled in and cooked first; the temperature is lowered gradually as smaller flavor grains are added, and then cooking is completed with the malts. This 6.5 hour, labor-intensive process is followed to capture the character and quality of each grain.

Distiller's Tasting Notes: Four Grain Straight Bourbon is aged for no less than three years and bottled at 95 proof. The barrel aging creates harmony between this complex whiskey and the vanilla and caramel notes from the 53-gallon, newly charred American white oak barrels to create a classic bourbon with Colorado character.

LEOPOLD BROS.

LEOPOLD BROS. is independently owned and, at twenty years, one of the oldest licensed distilleries operating in Colorado. They make some twenty different products, including bourbon, rye and specialty whiskeys, gin, liqueur and vodka, fernet, absinthe and aperitivo. They distribute widely in Colorado and sell products in approximately twenty other states, as well as internationally.

Philosophy: Leopold Bros. ferments and distills their spirits in house, and they are perhaps the only distillery in Colorado that malts their own barley on site. They source ingredients from Colorado farms, and they don't use artificial components.

The company also has a longstanding commitment to support its community, donating, for example, the net proceeds from facility tours to local, non-profit organizations.

Owners Scott and Todd Leopold are relatives of the renowned conservationist Aldo Leopold. The family tradition of commitment to environmental sustainability continues at the Leopold Bros. distillery, with production methods involving water conservation, composting and recycling.

Process & Product Notes: For their **Rocky Mountain Peach Whiskey**, Palisade peaches are de-stoned, macerated and blended with their whiskey. Next the blended spirit is aged in used barrels from their American Small Batch Whiskey. Notes of vanilla, raisin and oak are pulled from the barrel, and the spirit is naturally colored by the barrel and peach juice without the aid of artificial coloring agents.

In their **New York Apple Whiskey**, apples grown in New York state are pressed and blended with Leopold Bros. Whiskey. Finished

ADDRESS
5285 Joliet Street
Denver, Colorado 80239

OWNER(S)
Scott Leopold, Todd Leopold

CONTACT INFORMATION
303-307-1515
leopoldbros.com
facebook.com/leopoldbros

TASTING ROOM: Yes
TOURS: Yes

in charred American oak barrels, the spirit develops its natural coloration and crisp apple flavor with deep vanilla and caramel notes.

Rocky Mountain Blackberry Whiskey blends tart and sweet blackberries with their whiskey. It rests in charred American barrels, gaining notes of vanilla, raisin and oak for a richly complex finish.

FEATURED PRODUCT

Leopold Bros. **American Small Batch Whiskey,** with a traditional sour mash of corn and rye, is fermented in handmade American wooden tanks for a long period of time at cooler temperatures than industry standard. Todd Leopold, the head distiller, makes the first distillation through a Vendome copper pot still on grain to extract fuller and rounder flavors from the corn and rye. Then it is finished in a Carl column still.

The distillate is racked at 98 proof for the barrel to add subtle notes of oak and vanilla without overpowering the finished whiskey. It is bottled at 86 proof.

CRUSTA

- 1-1/2 oz Leopold Bros. American Small Batch Whiskey
- 3/4 oz Leopold Bros. American Orange Liqueur
- 1/2 oz Leopold Bros. Maraschino Liqueur
- 1/2 oz lemon juice
- 3 dashes bitters

Combine all ingredients in a cocktail shaker with ice. Shake until cold. Strain into a sugar-rimmed lowball glass. Garnish with a lemon twist.

Distiller's Tasting Notes: American Small Batch Whiskey has a grain-forward palate, with hay-like notes and a long, soft finish carrying hints of vanilla. Slow fermentation develops other subtle flavors in the whiskey, such as pear and raspberry.

LOCAL DISTILLING

LOCAL DISTILLING is a family-run business that produces vodka, gin, liqueur and a high-proof grain spirit. A corn whiskey is in development. They sell products in Colorado and Wisconsin.

Philosophy: "Our desire is to create libations that are high quality, can compete with large name brands and yet stay competitively priced," owner Jon Guelzow explains. "I believe with the resources available to us in Colorado we can achieve the quality necessary to not only compete but win over customers. We believe locally produced liquor products are the future."

Product & Process Notes: Local Distilling employs a proprietary silver filtration process, which they describe as a new technology to reduce or enhance certain characteristics of the finished product to achieve a smooth, crisp and clean flavor profile.

Local Distilling developed **Jory's Old Bird Gin** with a traditional gin profile. It is full-flavored with a balance of juniper, star anise and lemon peel.

Jory's Triple Sec is a triple-distilled orange liqueur made with real oranges and orange peels. They soak the product and make it in a small, custom copper still, which enables them to use half the typical sugar and no synthetic orange flavor.

Most gins are "dry" and categorized as London Dry, so Local Distilling decided to "buck the trend" and make **Jory's Sweet Gin**. A sweet gin called Old Tom predates London Dry. Old Tom was extremely popular during the 18th century—so popular that it

ADDRESS
417 Violet St
Golden, Colorado 80401

OWNER(S)
Jon Guelzow

CONTACT INFORMATION
720-708-2584
vanjakvodka.com
facebook.com/vanjakvodka

TASTING ROOM: Yes
TOURS: By appointment

caused a major wave of drunkenness across London in the early 1700s.

Jory's Sweet Gin is freshened with tones of lemongrass and light juniper. Especially recommended to fans of Moscato and worth the comparison with other modern versions of the Old Tom recipe.

FEATURED PRODUCT

Vanjak Vodka is a corn-based spirit with no added sugar or sweeteners. It is distilled six times, then silver and carbon filtered for a creamy smoothness. Fresh spring water from Eldorado Canyon is used to proof the vodka for bottling.

Tasting Notes: "We just say smooth and easy drinking," says Jon Guelzow, "but when we got a gold from *The 50 Best*, here is what they said—Nose: vanilla, cocoa, orange, light cream, cigar box, birch wood, clean. Palate: light vanilla, sugarcane, powdered sugar, syrup, creamy, pastry dough, grassy, mint, spicy, wet stone, light wood, balanced, smooth, silky, satisfying. Finish: vanilla, lemon drops, minty, peppery, grain, coffee, light, fragile, crisp, smooth."

TUFF MUDDER

- 1 oz Vanjak Vodka
- 1 oz chilled coffee
- 1 oz Kaluha
- 1/2 cup heavy cream
- 1 dash Angostura bitters
- 4 drops orange oil

Add coffee, Khalua, Vanjak to a shaker filled with ice. Stir. Strain into an old-fashioned glass. Add cream, garnish with bitters and 4 drops of orange oil.

MAD RABBIT DISTILLERY

MAD RABBIT Distillery products include bourbon, vodka, gin and rum, which they distribute in Colorado, mainly in the Front Range corridor.

Philosophy: Mad Rabbit follows a "grain-to-glass" ethos of making their spirits at their facility and using local ingredients where possible. All the mixers for their tasting room cocktails are made in house, and they strive to make the experiences of their customers memorable.

Co-owner and distiller Paul Page prizes this hands-on approach as a tradition that he is carrying forward from his grandfather and great-grandfather, who took pride in the quality of their moonshine "sweet water." "My grandpa and his dad had a still in their basement until one day when they literally blew a hole in the kitchen floor. Then, Grandma said 'no more stills!' Distilling might have skipped a generation but I have picked up and carried on the 'spirit' of my ancestors."

Process & Product Notes: Bravo Zulu - Triple Filtered Vodka is distilled from corn and bottled at 80 proof. It is smooth up front with a little corn sweetness on the back.

Bravo Zulu - V.I. Rum is distilled from cane molasses and bottled at 80 proof. It is sweet up front and has a smooth finish from the molasses.

ADDRESS
10860 Dover Street, Suite 2000
Westminster, Colorado 80021

OWNER(S)
Paul Page, Margaret Gutierrez

CONTACT INFORMATION
303-623-7222
madrabbitdistillery.com
facebook.com/madrabbitdistillery

TASTING ROOM: Yes
TOURS: By appointment

Bravo Zulu - Rocky Mountain Gin begins with their triple-filtered corn-base vodka for a smooth combination of two distinct styles of gin. It is bottled at 84 proof.

Featured Product

Bravo Zulu - Straight Bourbon Whiskey uses malted barley and non-GMO Olathe sweet corn from Colorado's Western Slope. It is aged a minimum of three years in new American white oak barrels and bottled at 86 proof.

Distiller's Tasting Notes: From silo to bottle, the bourbon is delicately produced to ensure the most enjoyable flavors and smooth finish that is expected from a premium quality spirit. The Straight Bourbon Whiskey has tastes at the front of sweet caramel and brown sugar. Hints of chocolate and vanilla flavors can be identified during the smooth bourbon finish.

Vodka Soda

So smooth you'll wonder why you added soda.

- 1-1/2 oz Bravo Zulu Vodka
- 1 lime wedge
- Ice

Poured over ice in a pint glass. Top with fresh club soda and garnish with a lime wedge. Enjoy!

MILE HIGH SPIRITS

MILE HIGH Spirits produces bourbon and specialty whiskeys, gin, vodka, rum and tequila (sourced-spirit from Mexico). They also have developed a roomy lounge at the distillery as an events venue with DJs, live music and patio games, as well as a cocktail bar. Their products are distributed in Colorado and New Mexico.

Philosophy: Mile High Spirits was begun with the goal of producing premium spirits, while sourcing the finest ingredients and offering buyers a fair price. Their ethic is to work hard to provide tasty spirits while having a great time in the process. Creating an active social scene and events venue at the distillery therefore has been a significant aspect of their business. Their slogan: "At Mile High Spirits we take our booze seriously, but not ourselves!"

Process & Product Notes: Fireside Peach was inspired by the popularity of peach-infused bourbon cocktails in their Denver tasting room. To capture that experience in a bottle, Colorado Palisade peaches are combined with their 80-proof Fireside Bourbon, resulting in a robust whiskey with subtle peach notes on the nose and palate, while maintaining the solid flavor and strength of the bourbon.

Elevate Vodka is distilled six times from non-GMO corn and bottled with filtered Rocky Mountain water for a crisp, smooth taste that can be enjoyed on the rocks or straight up.

ADDRESS
2201 Lawrence Street
Denver, Colorado 80205

OWNER(S)
Wyn Ferrell, Joe Von Feldt,
Chase Campbell

CONTACT INFORMATION
303-296-2226
drinkmhs.com
facebook.com/MileHighSpirits

TASTING ROOM: Yes
TOURS: Yes

Punching Mule, labelled "America's first canned Moscow Mule," begins with Mile High Spirits' Elevate Vodka. They add their ginger beer recipe, sweetened with beet sugar, along with natural lime flavor. After a full day of blending, the mix of natural ingredients chills for 24 hours. Just before canning, a precise amount of CO_2 is injected for a clean, crisp cocktail.

FEATURED PRODUCT

Fireside Bourbon has a mash with Colorado corn, rye and American-sourced barley, which is fermented with home-grown yeast. It is distilled in Mile High's custom copper still and aged in #3 char American white oak barrels.

Distiller's Tasting Notes: Fireside Bourbon has a toasted oak aroma that fills the nose, while smoky caramel and vanilla notes rest on the palate. The bourbon then has a smooth and robust finish.

FIRESIDE BOURBON SMASH

Think you don't like whiskey cocktails? Give this one a try! Like a julep, but with some lemon.

- 2 oz Fireside Bourbon
- 3/4 oz simple syrup
- 1/2 lemon, cut into wedges
- 4 mint leaves
- 1 mint sprig

In a mixing glass, muddle the lemon, mint leaves and simple syrup. Add Fireside Bourbon and fill with ice. Shake until chilled. Double-strain into an ice-filled rocks glass. Garnish with the mint sprig. No need for a straw.

Also try using Fireside Peach in place of Fireside Bourbon. Step it up with a few pieces of seasonal fruit, like blackberries or Palisade peaches.

RISING SUN DISTILLERY

RISING SUN Distillery is one of the few certified organic distilleries in Colorado. They make whiskey, gin, vodka, liqueur and brandy. Their products are distributed in Colorado.

Philosophy: Rising Sun takes pride in crafting their spirits completely in house, with custom-built batch distilling equipment and organic local ingredients. "All of our spirits are made from the highest quality grains, fruits and spices grown on family farms by farmers we have long-standing relationships with. Our fruit is processed by hand, our grains are mashed and fermented in house."

Process & Product Notes: **Rising Sun Organic Vodka** uses stone-ground 100-percent organic Kansas yellow corn in a step-down mashing technique that allows close control of sweetness drawn from the corn.

Rising Sun ferments directly on the mash for greater flavor, and once fermentation is complete, the vodka is distilled in a small-batch copper finishing still. They precisely draw off prime cuts of the spirit and further polish it with active-carbon filtering. The result is a smooth, clear and gluten-free vodka with a premium, slightly sweet finish.

For their **Organic Silk Road Gin**, Rising Sun distills 100-percent organic Kansas corn. Then they hand-grind organic herbs and spices and cold-steep them several days in the organic spirit base. Coriander, citrus, cardamom, juniper and fennel are some of the spices that add depth and character. The gin goes into a pot still for its final distillation. It delivers multiple taste layers with a soft botanical nose, herbal pallet and soft juniper finish.

ADDRESS
1330 Zuni Street #J
Denver, Colorado 80204

OWNER(S)
Dawn Richardson, Sol Richardson

CONTACT INFORMATION
303-534-1788
risingsundistillery.com
facebook.com/risingsundistilleryllc

TASTING ROOM: Yes
TOURS: Yes

Rising Sun creates its **Colorado Peach Brandy** with peaches from the Cox family farm in Palisade. After fermentation, the peach wine is distilled into a balanced eau de vie, then matured on oak for several months.

It is checked regularly until ready to bottle, when the color darkens and the peach is enhanced by the vanilla of the oak. The brandy has a subtle peach flavor with notes of vanilla and toast.

FEATURED PRODUCT

The **Colorado Chili Liqueur** begins with their Chili Spirit, made with Colorado ingredients using Old World schnapps-making techniques. Fresh Colorado-grown Anaheim chilies are hand processed and cold steeped in an in-house organic and gluten-free corn whiskey.

The Chili Spirit is distilled, with small-batch cuts taken at a moderate alcohol level for the fullest chili flavor, and then steeped a final time with dried Hatch Chilies. Organic agavé syrup is blended to finish the liqueur.

CLASSIC NEGRONI

A truly classic cocktail with colors of the rising sun.

- 1 oz Organic Silk Road Gin
- 1 oz sweet vermouth
- 1 oz Campari liqueur
- 1 Orange peel, for garnish

In a mixing glass, stir all liquid ingredients well with ice. Strain into a chilled cocktail glass, garnish with the orange peel and serve.

Distiller's Tasting Notes: Colorado Chili Liqueur has the initial earthy sweetness of the agave with the mildly spicy chili warming the palate on the finish, in a pleasing marriage of sweet and spice.

ROCKER SPIRITS

ROCKER SPIRITS produces two whiskeys, a vodka and a rum, with rye and wheat whiskeys in process. Their products are distributed in Colorado, and their tasting room offers a large menu of innovative cocktails using their spirits.

All their products are packaged in an award-winning bottle, uniquely designed to be rolled on its side when pouring the spirit and, when released, to roll itself back onto its base, hence the Rocker brand.

Philosophy: Rocker Spirits embraces innovation, but with a reverence for time-honored traditions of craftsmanship. Their unique bottle design displays this fusion of disruptive insight grounded in a deep regard for hand-made workmanship. Challenging to manufacture, its functional design was inspired by a 1930s oil can discovered by co-founder Duston Evans.

Duston has cast the spirit of their business in this way: "We're building a loyal tribe of mavericks seeking an original look, feel and experience."

Process & Product Notes: Their **Rocker Vodka**, bottled at 80 proof, is made with 100-percent corn grown outside Burlington in eastern Colorado. Filtered five to six times through activated charcoal from coconut husks, it is mostly odorless, with very mild grain and sweet notes and a clean mouthfeel.

Rocker Whiskey, with a mash bill of 70% corn and 30% wheat sourced from eastern Colorado, is aged at least three years in #3 Char new American oak barrels and bottled at 96 proof. A sweeter young whiskey with a creamy cereal nose, it presents flavors of

ADDRESS
5587 S. Hill Street
Littleton, Colorado 80120

OWNER(S)
Duston Evans, Patrick Johnson

CONTACT INFORMATION
303-795-7928
rockerspirits.com
facebook.com/rockerspirits

TASTING ROOM: Yes
TOURS: Yes

caramel, butterscotch and honey, and a long warm, moderate oak finish with notes of citrus.

The 86-proof **Rocker Rum** is produced with 100-percent sugar cane products and without additional sugar, herbs, fruits, spices or carbon filtering. Aged for six years in used whiskey barrels, adding oak and vanilla to the molasses and tropical fruit nose, the rum has flavors of light brown sugar, dried fruits and oak, with a lasting white pepper finish.

FEATURED PRODUCT

Rocker's **Port Finished Bourbon Whiskey**, like their Whiskey, has a heavily wheated mash bill, lending additional sweetness to the bourbon. All the grains are grown in eastern Colorado.

The bourbon is aged for at least three years in 53-gallon, #3 char, new white American oak barrels.

INVITING LIGHT

- 1 oz Rocker Whiskey
- 1 oz Rocker Rum
- 1 oz fresh lemon juice
- 3/4 oz chai tea syrup*
- 3/4 oz coconut milk
- 1/4 oz Corvus coffee chicory concentrate
- 1 dash Angostura bitters
- Garnish: Ground coffee & lemon peel

Place all mix ingredients in cocktail a shaker with ice. Shake lightly for ten seconds. Strain into a large rocks glass with crushed ice and garnish with ground coffee, a lemon peel and flowers if you're feeling fancy.
* Use Chai tea to make 1:1 ratio simple syrup.

Blender's Tasting Notes: The port-finished bourbon is very approachable, with a soft nose of vanilla, sweet corn and raisins. It presents flavors of bittersweet chocolate, pepper and dried dark fruits, and finishes warm, with lingering port, leather and toasted-oak notes.

STATE 38 DISTILLING

STATE 38 Distilling makes bourbon, malt, rye and wheat whiskeys, agave spirits with three levels of aging (blanco, reposado and añjeo), as well as gin and vodka, both based on agavé. Their products are distributed in Colorado, Nevada and Tennessee.

Philosophy: State 38 holds firmly to the virtues of hand crafting small-batch spirits using only organic or locally sourced ingredients. The made-from-scratch ethic extends as well to their equipment. "We hand made all our equipment," explains founder Sean Smiley. "And we obsess about the quality of raw materials, water and barrels." They also work to promote and celebrate their community, even naming the company after the 38th state of the union—Colorado.

Process & Product Notes: Scottish Peat Smoked Whisky uses grains sourced from the Islay region of Scotland where they are peat smoked, creating a soft oak nose with a vibrant peat smoke front and rich chocolate finish.

State 38 hand mills each batch of grain, which is fermented in small, 250-gallon tanks. It is double distilled, first "on the grain"—a process where the grain is not separated from the wort after mashing, but is retained throughout the fermenting and distilling process—to carry the rich grain flavor into the distilled spirit. Then it's aged in new American white oak barrels with oak staves hand selected for a strong caramel, vanilla and cinnamon flavor profile.

Their **Rocky Mountain Straight Rye Whiskey** is made with Colorado-sourced rye grains that are fermented and distilled on-

---

ADDRESS
400 Corporate Circle, Suite B
Golden, Colorado 80401

OWNER(S)
Sean Smiley

CONTACT INFORMATION
720-242-7219
state38.com
facebook.com/State38Distilling

TASTING ROOM: Yes
TOURS: Yes

the-grain. This straight rye whiskey has a distinctive fig and dark cherry finish with subtle spice.

State 38 **Straight Wheat Whiskey** also is fermented and distilled on the grain for distinct flavor using local Colorado wheat grains. The whiskey is light and floral, leaving a fresh finish.

FEATURED PRODUCT

Loveday Colorado Bourbon is produced using many of the same methods as for their Scottish Peat Smoked Whisky. Each batch of bourbon grain, which includes malt grain in the mash bill, is hand milled and fermented in small, 250-gallon tanks.

Head distiller and owner Sean Smiley double distills the whiskey, the first time on the grain to maintain the grain flavors. It then ages for two years in new American white oak barrels, Char #3, medium toast, cooper select.

SMOKED OLD FASHIONED

A non-traditional take on a standard whiskey cocktail, using the State 38 peat-smoked whiskey rather than bourbon or rye whiskey to impart subtle smoky notes to the drink.

- 1-1/2 oz Scottish Peat Smoked Whiskey
- 1 dash Angostura bitters
- 1 dash chocolate bitters
- 1 dash cherry bitters
- 1 dash orange bitters
- 1 sugar cube

Mix ingredients and add a dash or two of water to taste.

Distiller's Tasting Notes: Loveday Colorado Bourbon has a sweet, smooth palate with a mellow oak background in the bourbon profile. The oak barrel staves are hand picked for a strong caramel, vanilla and cinnamon flavor profile. And the medium char provides the right amount of smoke finish. The malt grains help impart a rich chocolate and caramel to the finish.

STRANAHAN'S ROCKY MOUNTAIN SINGLE MALT WHISKEY

STRANAHAN'S, FOUNDED in 2004, was the first modern micro-distillery licensed in Colorado. It has since grown to be the largest and probably the most widely recognized. Owned since 2010 by Proximo Distillers, Stranahan's produces only malt whiskey, which is distributed nationally.

Philosophy: Stranahan's standard is meticulous management for the highest quality. As master distiller Rob Dietrich explains, "The beauty of hand-producing each batch of our single-malt whiskey from barley to bottle is that we have our fingerprints on the process every step of the way. Using only the finest resources, our whiskey is made from four ingredients: 100-percent malted barley, yeast, Rocky Mountain water and time in the barrel."

Process & Product Notes: Stranahan's produces small-batch American single-malt whiskey in four expressions: Original, Diamond Peak, Sherry Cask and Snowflake.

The whiskey is non-chill filtered. And each barrel is bottled by hand. Their bottles carry no age statement because the whiskeys are aged in new oak and monitored by batch.

As explained by Rob Dietrich, "The Scotch industry uses used barrels and that's why it's so important for them to declare an age statement—because it takes longer for Scotch whisky to pull all the flavors from a used barrel."

Stranahan's Sherry Cask is made with their four-year-old Rocky Mountain Single Malt Whiskey, which is finished in used 500-liter Sherry Oloroso casks from Spain. The whiskey's vanilla,

ADDRESS
200 S. Kalamath St.
Denver, Colorado 80223

OWNER(S)
Proximo Distillers, LLC

CONTACT INFORMATION
303-296-7440
stranahans.com
facebook.com/stranahans.colorado.whiskey

TASTING ROOM: Yes
TOURS: Yes

caramel, dark chocolate and depth of oak melds with the rich, fruity notes of the sherry cask to create a flavor profile of unusual depth and complexity.

The **Diamond Peak** expression is strictly 4-year-old single-malt whiskey that is hand selected by the master distiller from among the most distinct casks. It shares flavor notes of Turkish apricot, dark roast coffee, butterscotch oak, cayenne and Mexican hot chocolate, with a rolling, creamy finish.

Stranahan's Snowflake, a limited offering, is a custom, single-barrel blend, meaning each year's batch is unique like a snowflake.

Snowflake begins with Stranahan's Original, and over the course of eighteen months it is finished in casks from all over the world that have previously been filled with different whiskeys.

Each year's batch spends a different amount of time in different casks, so the flavor results change every year.

FEATURED PRODUCT

Stranahan's Original Whiskey is a marriage of their single-malt whiskey that has been aged for two, three, four and five years in standard 53-gallon new American white oak barrels with a #3 char.

Distiller's Tasting Notes: Stranahan's Original boasts flavor notes of cinnamon-butter, vanilla, chocolate, warm caramel and spiced pear. It finishes with notes of cayenne, rich tobacco, oak and aged leather.

WHISTLING HARE DISTILLERY

WHISTLING HARE is a family-owned and operated small-batch distillery. Their products include bourbon and rye whiskey, gin, white and aged rum, and vodka. They serve their tasting room visitors seasonal offerings and not-yet released spirits like a single-malt whiskey that they currently are maturing. Their products are distributed in Colorado.

Philosophy: Whistling Hare was founded to make fine spirits for Colorado's outdoor lifestyle that are rooted in the land. Their namesake mascot is the American Pica, a familiar resident in the alpine Rockies, also called a whistling hare.

They started from the premise that quality spirits should be made from fresh, local and sustainable ingredients. The qualities and traditional values of whiskey and whiskey-making in Scotland are another inspiration for Whistling Hare founder Sandy Rothe, who studied there under a master distiller.

Process & Product Notes: Whistling Hare's **Blue Corn Vodka** is made from 100-percent blue corn, resulting in a flavorful vodka with distinct character of grain and a smooth, subtly sweet finish that can be enjoyed on its own or added for a distinctive character in mixed drinks.

Whistling Hare White Rum has a recipe of premium molasses and evaporated cane juice. Reminiscent of a full-bodied Caribbean-style rum, it is smooth and easy to sip or mix in cocktails.

Wine Barrel Rum is produced as the pride of their rum fleet. Aged for over a year in French red wine casks, the award-winning rum is a premium spirit recommended for sipping on the rocks.

ADDRESS
7655 W. 108th Avenue, Unit 400
Westminster, Colorado 80021

OWNER(S)
Sandy Rothe

CONTACT INFORMATION
720-335-6009
whistlinghare.com
facebook.com/whistlinghare

TASTING ROOM: Yes
TOURS: By appointment

Featured Product

Whistling Hare Blue Corn Bourbon is made solely from non-GMO blue corn grown by the Ute Mountain Ute Tribe in southwest Colorado. All the corn is harvested and milled on the reservation.

After mashing, the blue corn wash is fermented using fine yeasts selected for rich flavors that can stand years of barrel aging. Head distiller Sandy Harrison double distills each batch in a 250-gallon pot still with a copper column and cuts are made by hand.

The bourbon matures in charred new American oak barrels. Initially these were mostly 25-gallon barrels, but now 53-gallon barrels are used. They are also experimenting with spiral-cut and wave-stave barrels for greater surface area to enrich and accelerate flavoring.

Bison Grass Cocktail

- 1-1/2 oz Blue Corn Bourbon
- 1/2 oz honey simple syrup
- 1/2 oz lemon juice
- 1 oz ginger beer
- 3-4 basil leaves
- Ice

Muddle 3 basil leaves (2 if they're large) with syrup and lemon juice in a shaker. Add bourbon and ice and shake. Strain into a rocks glass and add ginger beer. Fill glass with ice and garnish with a medium sized basil leaf.

Distiller's Tasting Notes: Blue Corn Bourbon starts with a big corn and oak nose with hints of spice and nuts. The smooth palate has tastes of allspice, chocolate, orange and cherry atop big, nutty blue corn flavors. Adding ice or water opens up the more subtle flavors for sipping or for a tasty Old Fashion.

COLORADO: SOUTHEAST AREA

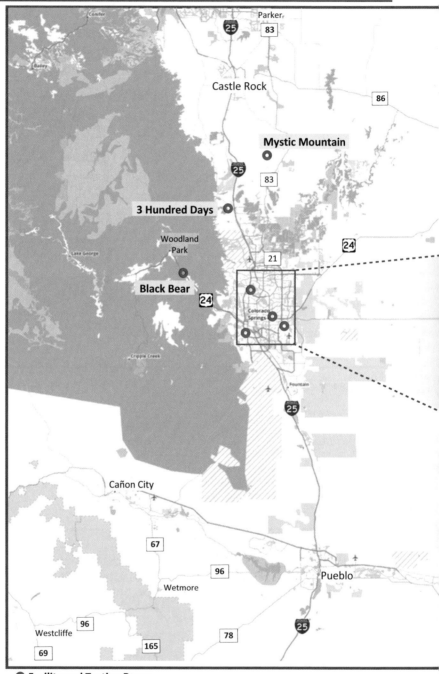

⦿ Facility and Tasting Room

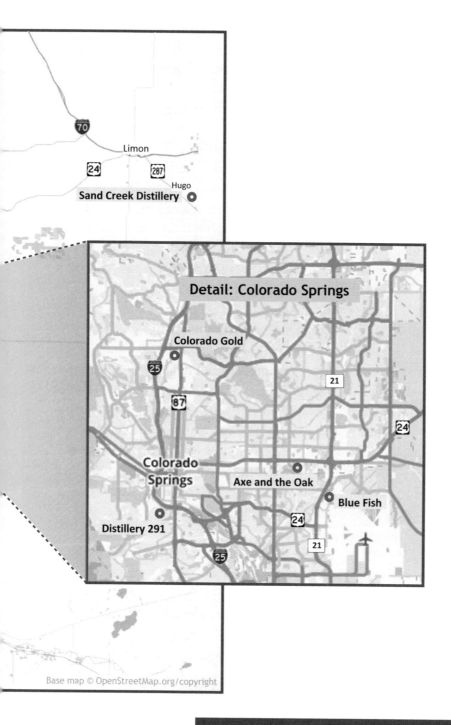

Limon

Hugo

Sand Creek Distillery

Detail: Colorado Springs

Colorado Gold

Colorado Springs

Axe and the Oak

Blue Fish

Distillery 291

3 Hundred Days Distilling

IN THEIR diverse Western Sippin' Shine product line, 3 Hundred Days Distilling currently produces eight infused and flavored new-make or moonshine whiskey products. Bottled in Mason jars they are "ready to drink." They also produce an aged whiskey called Centennial Wheat. Their whiskeys are sold throughout Colorado.

Philosophy: Owner and distiller Michael Girard says his company's products are inspired by Colorado's storied history of bootlegging moonshine, as well as its ingenuity and entrepreneurial spirit. Girard also wants his customers to understand that although the term moonshine technically indicates an illegal product, every product produced at 3 Hundred Days is completely legal! And as a "Colorado Proud" member company, 3 Hundred Days promotes locally-grown and produced agricultural products.

Exemplifying bootleg ingenuity, Girard made his first run of moonshine in Afghanistan in 2010, where he was serving as an explosive ordnance disposal technician removing and disposing of Improvised Explosive Devices (IEDs) and roadside bombs. His first still was made from a pressure cooker used in an IED, and the first mash bill was root beer, he explains, "cause that's all I had."

Process & Product Notes: The eight **Western Sippin' Shine** new-make whiskeys are infused with juices, sugar, honey or other botanicals , creating products flavored like apple pie, peach cobbler, margarita, strawberry lemonade, southern sweet tea, and honey.

Their **Firebomb Shine** is 100-proof new-make infused with highly concentrated cinnamon to create a fireball jawbreaker taste, "that one-of-a-kind burn for the kid in all of us."

ADDRESS	CONTACT INFORMATION
279 Beacon Lite Rd #G	719-466-0023
Monument, CO 80132	3hundreddays.com
	facebook.com/3hundreddaysofshine
OWNER(S)	
Michael Girard	TASTING ROOM: By appointment
	TOURS: Yes

Historically, Colorado moonshiners made a distinctive shine from sugar and sugar beets called Sugar Moon. This idea could have come to Colorado from Tennessee, where a common moonshine mash bill was 70-percent cane sugar and 30-percent corn and wheat shorts (roughly milled wheat brand, germ and flour). Regardless of the historical beginning, with that inspiration, 3 Hundred Days produces a 105-proof white whiskey called **Sugar Moon**.

Featured Product

Centennial Wheat Whiskey, also in 3 Hundred Days' Western Sippin' Shine family, is distilled from sugar and wheat. It is aged in 10-gallon white oak barrels and infused with complex aromas and flavorings.

MOONSHINE MOJITO

- 2 oz Margarita Moon Shine
- 2 oz lemonade
- 2 oz fresh slapped mint

Mix in equal parts for a refreshing combination of lemon and mint with the lime of Margarita Moon Shine.

Distillers Tasting Notes: The barrel aging and complex infusions give the 80-proof Centennial Wheat moonshine a smoother and rich, full flavor with notes of cane and bourbon.

AXE AND THE OAK DISTILLERY

THE FOUNDERS of Axe and the Oak have held to a vision of creating delicious local whiskeys "that don't cost you an arm and a leg." They began with a bourbon and now also offer rye and white whiskeys, a forthcoming coffee liqueur, as well as other specialty whiskeys. Their products are available in Colorado, with their specialty whiskeys most likely to be found at their Whiskey House in Colorado Springs.

Philosophy: Co-owner Casey Ross underscores community as a core value for their business. "From day one," he explains, "our goal has been to create a whiskey you want to share with friends. For us that means buying our grains from a local farmer, building our own stills, making our bourbon by hand, and treating our friends like they're family." Therefore their tasting room, The Whiskey House, figures prominently in their business. After three years of marketing their bourbon to enthusiastic customers, "it was time to open a tasting room. But this couldn't be a run-of-the-mill tasting room," Casey emphasizes. "It had to be a place for people to look each other in the eye and have an engaging conversation. We hope you'll experience more than good whiskey—we hope you'll find warmth, good times and community."

Process & Product Notes: Their recently released **Pike's Peak Hill Shine** was, in a way, "discovered." While making their bourbon and tasting the shine right off the still, they loved it and decided it deserved to be bottled in its own right. Cut to 104 proof, this moonshine has flavors of buttered toast and dates.

ADDRESS
Whiskey House
1604 S. Cascade Ave
Colorado Springs, CO 80905

OWNER(S)
Jason Jackson, Casey Ross,
Scott White, Eric Baldini

CONTACT INFORMATION
719-660-1624
axeandtheoak.com
facebook.com/axeandtheoakwhiskeyhouse

TASTING ROOM: Yes
TOURS: By appointment

Colorado Mountain Incline Rye was released at the end of 2017 as their flagship rye whiskey. They also produce a companion blended rye. Bottled at 98 proof, both ryes have a sweet, peppery character.

Featured Product

Axe and the Oak Bourbon has from the beginning been the company's flagship product. Head distiller Jason Dale Jackson uses corn and rye from Ravenkamp and Hollowell Farms in Eastern Colorado. Product distillation occurs just four times per week, "slow and low" to preserve flavor in the whiskey. Aged in new American white oak barrels, char #4, the bourbon is released in batches several times each year.

Following record sales of their bourbon in 2016, they transitioned to a blended spirit in 2017, aging their original product even longer and then combining it with a sourced bourbon. With this carefully blended product they are striving to maintain the award-winning qualities of their bourbon while serving an expanding community of fans.

TOBACCO OLD FASHIONED

- 2 oz Axe and the Oak Bourbon
- 1/2 oz maple simple syrup*
- 4 dashes Angostura bitters
- 1 tsp pipe tobacco
- 1 tsp cracked nutmeg
- 1 orange peel
- 1 large ice sphere

Add bourbon, syrup, bitters, nutmeg and tobacco to a mixing glass. Stir until cooled. Pour through a fine mesh strainer into a rocks glass over an ice sphere. Garnish with flamed orange peel. *Recipe by Jacob Pfund.*

*Maple simple syrup: Mix 2 parts maple syrup, 1 part hot water.

Distiller's Tasting Notes: Axe and the Oak Bourbon blends aromas of vanilla, butterscotch and caramel. The palate carries flavors of maple, apple, caramel, clove and tobacco. Its finish is smooth, with lingering caramel.

BLACK BEAR DISTILLERY

BLACK BEAR Distillery spirits include bourbon, corn, malt and white whiskeys and rum. Their flagship spirit is a special Irish-style whiskey. The products are distributed in Colorado.

Philosophy: Victor Matthews, the owner and head distiller, is dedicated to artisan, micro-craft spirits, honoring his family heritage of distilling, and using all non-GMO, natural Colorado small-farm products—including heirloom grains, from producers that he knows personally. His still is American-made, as are bottles, labels and wooden corks, all made locally when possible.

Black Bear also strives for sustainable and "green" operations. Solar panels and generator provide power to their grinder and pumps, and used grains go back to local farmers to feed livestock. "We are not there yet," Matthews explains, "but our goal is to eventually leave the grid entirely and function as a completely sustainable and green legacy producer."

Process & Product Notes. Black Bear's **MountainShine** was created after two years of work to capture the rich color and flavor of his grandfather's original corn whiskey from the Blue Ridge Mountains.

Victor Matthews emphasizes that "this is not the common product that tastes like vodka or Everclear." An essential difference, he explains, is distillation in one low-slow run, which produces a smooth and distinctively flavorful product. A companion spirit is MountainShine Reserve. Warm, fragrant and golden, it is aged for approximately six months in charred barrels.

ADDRESS
10375 Ute Pass Ave.
Green Mountain Falls, CO 80819

OWNER(S)
Victor Matthews

CONTACT INFORMATION
719-964-2990
BlackBearDistillery.com
facebook.com/BlackBearDistillery

TASTING ROOM: Yes
TOURS: Yes

Black Bear Rum, distilled from brown sugar and molasses with their one-slow-run technique for rich flavors, is then barrel-aged for three to six months in second-use charred American oak, imbuing it with additional flavors and a light golden color.

Black Bear Vodka, a wheat and corn spirit, is made from the 50 to 80 proof tails produced by the low-slow distilling process for their other spirits. These tails go through a second distillation to produce an extremely clean and flavorful vodka high in alcohol, which is cut and bottled at 80 proof.

Featured Product

Black Bear Irish Style Whiskey, made with local ingredients, adheres with such fidelity to the traditional methods and style of Irish whiskey that it is the only American spirit officially approved by the U.S. and Ireland to be labeled "Irish Style." Those traditional methods and styles include use of malted and un-malted barley, corn, multiple stills and smoke-free fire.

IRISH CHERRY MANHATTAN

This cocktail combines the beauty of an Irish Style Whiskey Manhattan, the sweetness of cherry, and the sophistication of a splash of brandy.

- 2 oz Irish Style Whiskey
- 1 oz fresh sweet vermouth
- 1 oz cherry brandy
- 2 dashes Peychaud's bitters
- 1/2 oz juice of premium cherries

Mix whiskey, sweet vermouth, brandy, cherry juice and bitters. Add ice and shake vigorously. Strain into a chilled martini glass with single cherry.

Distiller's Tasting Notes: Distilled with a single-run, low-slow pot still for deeper corn flavor, the Irish Style Whiskey matures in first-use charred American oak cask for one year, with additional sherry staves. The traditional mash bill, distillation methods and aging create a fine whiskey with flavors of caramel, oak and rich citrus toffee.

BLUE FISH DISTILLERY

B LUE FISH Distillery arose from a lifelong connection that co-owner and head distiller John Fisher has had with distilled spirits and distilling. As a child at his grandmother's house, he was fascinated by an empty bottle of Fisch's Bitters—blue in color with the shape of a fish. In high school, he experimented with distilling moonshine, following instructions from a library book. The allure continued through his career as a mechanical engineer, and years later, during a business trip to China, he purchased a blown-glass still, just because he thought "it was pretty cool."

When many years later he unexpectedly received the empty Fisch's bottle in the mail from his grandmother, John took it as a sign to pursue his dream and begin a new career and distillery business. Launched in December 2014, it naturally was named Blue Fish. Today the distillery makes whiskeys, rum, vodka and an agavé spirit. Blue Fish products currently are sold in Colorado, primarily in the Colorado Springs area and at their distillery.

Philosophy: Blue Fish was founded as a craft, "grain to bottle" distillery, where mashing, fermenting, distilling and bottling are performed at their distillery. "My goal is to produce small runs of fine spirits to be enjoyed with friends and family," John explains. "While we make a lot of white spirits, I aim to make them all good enough to sip on ice, if you are in the mood, or mix them to make your favorite cocktail."

Process & Product Notes: Their **first single-barrel bourbon** batch sold out. The second barrel is scheduled for release by second quarter 2018. Its mash bill is 55% corn, 30% barley and 15% oat and is aged in 15-gallon new American oak barrels.

ADDRESS	**CONTACT INFORMATION**
5745 Industrial Place, Suite A	719-574-2038
Colorado Springs, CO 80916	bluefishdistillery.com
	facebook.com/bluefishdistillery
OWNER(S)	
John Fisher, Ellen Fisher	**TASTING ROOM:** Yes
	TOURS: Yes

Blue Fish's **Pikes Peak Clear** is a moonshine with distinct corn flavor that is good on ice or as a mixer.

Their **American White Rum**, good to sip or as a mixer, has a hint of molasses on the finish. At the Denver International Spirits Competition, the moonshine won a silver medal and the rum a bronze medal.

Featured Product

Blue Fish Vodka is a smooth spirit made from cane sugar and barley. Head distiller John Fisher distills the vodka twice—once in a pot still, with final distillation in a column to achieve 190+ proof. It is carbon filtered to remove any rough edges. The vodka, first produced in May 2016, has won a gold medal at the Denver International Spirits Competition.

Apple Pie Moonshine

Makes about 1/2 gallon at 40 proof. It doesn't *taste* strong, so be warned.

- 1 bottle Pikes Peak Clear
- 21 oz apple cider (suggest unfiltered)
- 1/2 can frozen apple juice
- 1-2 cinnamon stick

- 1/3 cup brown sugar
- 1/4 tsp nutmeg
- 1/4 tsp allspice
- 1/8 tsp ginger

Combine all ingredients except alcohol in a big pot. Heat to boiling, then cool. Once at room temperature add alcohol and bottle. Store in the fridge; it will get better with age. Remove cinnamon sticks after about two weeks, or once desired amount of cinnamon is reached.

Distiller's Tasting Notes: The combination of cane sugar and barley gives a clean spirit, while retaining a nice mouthfeel and sweet finish.

COLORADO GOLD DISTILLERY

COLORADO GOLD is one of the oldest distilleries in Colorado, and is dedicating itself now to producing premiere spirits into the future from a new 18,000 square-foot facility. They distill bourbon, corn and rye whiskeys, and their distinctive hemp-based vodka. Colorado Gold products are sold at locations in fourteen states, including Colorado and New Mexico, California, Florida, Georgia, Iowa, Louisiana, Minnesota, Nebraska, North Dakota, Oklahoma, Oregon, South Dakota and Texas.

Philosophy: Colorado Gold places quality above quantity. Their standard is being the best by distilling and finishing everything they sell. As owner Peter Caciola states regarding their innovative vodka, "I just wanted to make the best damn vodka I could."

Process & Product Notes: The **Colorado Gold Single-Barrel Straight Bourbon** is a four-grain, single-barrel, four-year-old expression. They use Colorado grains in their mash. It has won multiple gold medals and been lauded by Jimmy Murray's *Whisky Bible*. "Yet," Peter observes, true to their philosophy, "we produce less than twenty barrels a year and like it that way."

Their **Rocky Mountain Rye Whiskey** has a mash of 95% rye and 5% malted barley. Bottled at 90 proof and aged for two years, the expression is especially smooth for a rye, while retaining the signature spice flavors.

Colorado's Own Corn Whiskey is mashed from Colorado sweet corn and lightly aged in the distillery's own used bourbon barrels, which rounds off its sweet flavor and imparts a blonde color— giving it the nickname "Little Colorado Blonde Whiskey."

ADDRESS
4242 N. Nevada Avenue
Colorado Springs, CO 80907

OWNER(S)
Peter Caciola

CONTACT INFORMATION
719-260-5545
coloradohighvodka.com
facebook.com/ColoradoGoldSpirits

TASTING ROOM: Yes
TOURS: Yes

Colorado Gold offers a select barrel program where a retailer (or individual) selects a barrel exclusively for them and receives the spirit hand bottled at cask strength.

Featured Product

Colorado High Hemp Vodka is the only vodka in the country, the company reports, that is fermented and distilled from hemp as the base grain material, rather than just a flavor infusion. The mash is 51-percent organic hemp, plus Colorado corn, and yields a remarkably soft spirit. The vodka is further processed ten times through a carbon filtration system of their own design to polish the spirit's softness.

Distiller's Tasting Notes: Colorado High Hemp Vodka is a super-clean, easy-drinking vodka that delivers a luxurious mouthfeel from the natural oiliness of the hemp. There's no need to brace yourself for the typical vodka bite, because it's a mellow spirit that goes down smoothly. The finish is just as nice, with the organic hemp adding subtle sweetness and nuttiness.

COLORADO HIGH MOUNTAIN MULE

- 1-1/2 oz Colorado High Vodka
- 4 oz premium ginger beer
- 2 dashes Angostura bitters
- 1 lime

Mix Colorado High Vodka, ginger beer and bitters in the Moscow Mule mug. Finish with a squeeze of fresh lime juice and one wedge for garnish.

DISTILLERY 291

SITTING BELOW Pikes Peak and Cheyenne Mountain, Distillery 291 is a small-batch distillery that makes bourbon, malt, rye, white and specialty whiskeys, as well as liqueurs. Their products are distributed in Colorado and California.

Philosophy: Distillery 291 was founded by its owner and distiller, Michael Myers, to replicate the taste, smell and folklore of the Wild West. As a youth, he grew up in Georgia and Tennessee, in the heart of whiskey and horse country, where the names Daniels, Beam and Dickel were part of family life. He was surrounded by these traditions of whiskey-making and drinking, absorbing a deep regard for that history and culture and an enduring admiration for the rugged and rebellious cowboy West.

Process & Product Notes: To capture the character and values of traditional whiskey making, Distillery 291 adheres to a grain-to-bottle ethos, where all processes are performed in-house with small-batch production methods.

291 American Whiskey is distilled from a bourbon mash that is light-aged for three months in American white oak barrels and then mellowed with aspen charcoal. It has a unique fruit-and-floral flavor for sipping or mixing.

291 Colorado Rye Whiskey White Dog is a distinctly flavored but mellow, unaged rye whiskey. "During the very first run," Myers says he knew he'd struck gold when he "heard the still howl with this White Dog."

For their **291 Colorado Bourbon Whiskey**, the spirit is aged in American white oak with a deep char. It won double gold for Best

ADDRESS
1647 S. Tejon Street
Colorado Springs, CO 80905

OWNER(S)
Michael Myers

CONTACT INFORMATION
719-323-8010
distillery291.com
facebook.com/distillery291

TASTING ROOM: Yes
TOURS: Yes

Small-Batch Bourbon (Up to 5 Years) at the San Francisco World Spirits competition.

To top off an evening, The DECC, a citrus clove whiskey liqueur, is sweet and viscous, with a slight stickiness from clove simple syrup and citrus peels that go into the distillation run. At 70 proof it's warming, with beautiful botanical influence.

Featured Product

Distillery 291 Colorado Whiskey is a traditional whiskey made from rye malt sour mash and aged in 10-gallon American white oak barrels with a deep char. It is finished with toasted aspen staves.

This whiskey has won numerous awards and gold medals, including Best in Category for American Rye Whiskey, No Age Statement, in the 2016 World Whiskies Awards put on by *Whisky Magazine*.

---

291 COLORADO PEACH OLD FASHIONED

- 2 oz 291 Colorado Whiskey
- 1 oz raw sugar peach simple syrup
- 3 dashes black walnut bitters
- 2 dashes peach bitters
- 1 lemon twist
- Luxardo cherry or peach

Build in rocks glass and garnish with lemon twist and Luxardo Cherry or Peach. Fee Brothers bitters suggested.

Shown on cover of *Denver Life Magazine*.

Distiller's Tasting Notes: 291 Colorado Whiskey is full-bodied with strong notes of cinnamon, rye and oak, balanced with a subtle maple sweetness. It is sweet on the front and spicy in the middle, with a sweet finish.

MYSTIC MOUNTAIN DISTILLERY

MYSTIC MOUNTAIN grew from a family history, dating back to the 1800s and up through the end of Prohibition, of making moonshine in Colorado. With the repeal of Prohibition, the family recipes were locked away until 2004, when Fred Linneman revived the family tradition and founded the distillery outside of Larkspur. The current owners have continued and built on that legacy since purchasing the distillery in 2016, when Fred retired. They make bourbon, corn, moonshine and specialty whiskeys, gin and vodka. Their products are sold in Colorado and Wyoming, as well as Illinois and South Carolina.

Philosophy: Mystic Mountain upholds the moonshiner's tradition of serving the people, while expanding the variety of spirits it produces. "From our humble beginnings outside Cripple Creek, Colorado, in the late 1800s to now," master distiller Jonathon Nesvik affirms, "we truly believe that everyone should be able to enjoy premium quality spirits at a price they can afford."

Process & Product Notes: Rocky Mountain Sippin' Hooch Moonshine is made today just as it was back in the late 1800s and early 1900s—handcrafted in small batches, distilled slowly at lower temperatures and bottled at 101 proof with Rocky Mountain sweet water from their own deep underground well for time-tested quality and smooth taste. A silver-medal winner at the Denver International Spirits Competition.

Colorado Blue Vodka is a premium vodka distilled slowly at lower temperatures to achieve a clean, crisp taste. Bottled at 80 proof, it is very smooth with a rich body.

ADDRESS
11505 Spring Valley Rd.
Larkspur, CO 80118

TASTING ROOM (SEE NE-CO MAP)
12136 Grant Circle, Unit B
Thornton, CO 80241

OWNER(S)
Brad Lee Schroeder, Tracy Schroeder,
Jonathon Nesvik

CONTACT INFORMATION
303-663-9375
mmdistillery.com
facebook.com/MysticMountainDistillery
TASTING ROOM: YES
TOURS: No

Outlaw Red Cinnamon Whiskey is not a typical candy-coated cinnamon whiskey. Beginning with their premium Outlaw Whiskey, natural cinnamon and spices are infused with a careful balance of cinnamon and smooth premium whiskey. Bottled at 80 proof, Outlaw Red is one of the strongest cinnamon whiskeys sold. A two-time winner of a silver medal at the Denver International Spirits Competition.

Featured Product

Outlaw Whiskey is perfected from original family recipes and handcrafted in small batches with traditional methods, including slow distillation at lower temperatures for quality. The whiskey matures in new American oak barrels and, again following tradition, is aged by taste, not arbitrary time. "When it's ready," they say, "why wait?"

After passing through their custom filtration system, the whiskey is bottled with the sweet water from their deep underground well, helping give Outlaw Whiskey its smooth and mellow flavor.

WERTHER'S OUTLAW MARTINI

An amazing caramel drink that tastes just like a Werther's Original Candy.

- 2 oz Outlaw Whiskey
- 1 oz Smirnoff Caramel Vodka
- 1 oz DeKuyper Buttershots
- 1-1/4 oz Kahlua
- 5 drops half & half cream
- 1 splash Pepsi

Fill cocktail shaker with ice and add all ingredients. Shake well and pour into martini glass.

Distiller's Tasting Notes: Outlaw Whiskey presents woody aromas with a scent of caramel, faint anise pastry and spicy backdrop. Its smooth, medium body has tastes of oak, caramel, toasted nuts and a touch of vanilla. The finish is mellow and of good length, with licorice, buttercream and slight peppercorn elements. Winner of silver and bronze medals at the Denver International Spirits Competition.

SAND CREEK DISTILLERY

SAND CREEK Distillery, a veteran-owned craft distillery, produces malt whiskey, which is sold in Colorado.

Philosophy: Sand Creek Distilling was established by Lucas Hohl—not only with a passion to create fine spirits, but also to encourage agritourism, rural revitalization and entrepreneurship in and around his Eastern Colorado community of Hugo. "Sand Creek Distillery is the result of my insatiable desire to create something truly excellent from scratch," he explains. "And what my distillery lacks in size," he continues, "I make up for with enthusiasm and willingness to experiment."

Process & Products Notes: All Sand Creek Distillery products are completely hand-crafted in-house by one person, Lucas Hohl. He uses 100-percent malted barley as his grain bill, and it is mashed, stirred, lautered, sparged, fermented and distilled entirely by hand.

"Since I appreciate the subtle variations in each spirit run," Lucas explains, "I destroy the feints and do not add any to subsequent distillations. Through this process I am sacrificing consistency. But I believe I am escalating the quality and character of the whiskeys."

Whisky Distilled from Malt Mash, Sand Creek's second product, is being released in 2018. It is a single-malt style whiskey matured in second use barrels. The spirit presents a light character in flavor and mouthfeel.

ADDRESS
324 5th Street, Suite A
Hugo, CO 80821

OWNER(S)
Lucas N. Hohl

CONTACT INFORMATION
719-297-1022
sandcreekdistillery.com

TASTING ROOM: Yes
TOURS: Yes

Featured Product

Standard Single Malt Whisky, Sand Creek's primary product, has a grain bill of 100% malted barley. The whiskey is double-distilled in pot stills and the hearts are selected by nosing and tasting notes only.

The Standard Single Malt is matured in charred, new American oak barrels for at least 1 year. Sand Creek utilizes six- and fifteen-gallon barrels for aging. These small barrels permit a strong infusion of wood spice that normally is found in products with much longer maturation times.

The spirit is monitored throughout the aging process to ensure desired characteristics are developing and that no barrel will be bottled before it is ready.

The first barrel was bottled July 29, 2017, and the third barrel at the end of the following November.

BECKMAN

Named after moonshiner brothers of local legend, who had fine taste but dressed modestly.

- 1-1/2 oz Standard Single Malt
- 4 oz ginger ale
- 1/4 oz grenadine
- 1 cherry (or mint)
- Ice

Pour ginger ale into either a tumbler (ice cubes) or highball glass (crushed ice). Next, add Standard Single Malt Whiskey and then the grenadine. Quick stir and serve with cocktail straw and a mint or cherry garnish.

Distiller's Tasting Notes: The Standard Single Malt has a bourbon-like mouthfeel. It is mellow, with caramel and fig first notes that blend with a rye-like wood spice.

Colorado: Northwest Area

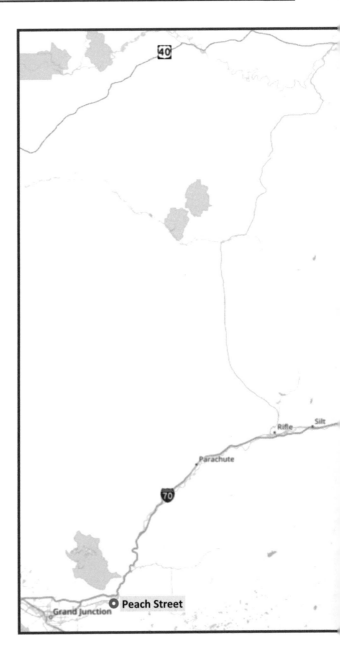

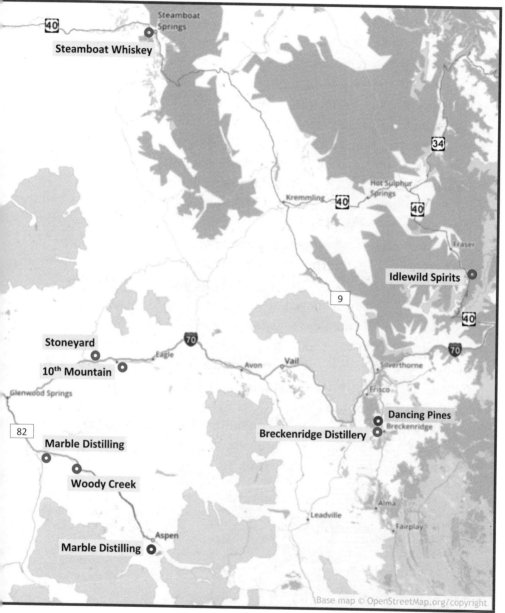

40

Steamboat Springs

Steamboat Whiskey

34

Hot Sulphur Springs

Kremmling 40

40

Fraser

Idlewild Spirits ⦿

9

40

70

Stoneyard
⦿
Eagle

10th Mountain ⦿

Avon   Vail   Silverthorne

Glenwood Springs

Frisco

82

Dancing Pines
⦿
Breckenridge

Breckenridge Distillery ⦿

Marble Distilling
⦿

Woody Creek
⦿

Alma

Leadville

Fairplay

Aspen
Marble Distilling ⦿

Base map © OpenStreetMap.org/copyright

⦿ Facility and Tasting Room   ⦿ Tasting Room Only

10TH MOUNTAIN WHISKEY & SPIRIT COMPANY

LOCATED IN Gypsum, just west of Vail, the 10th Mountain Whiskey & Spirit Company was founded in the name of the 10th Light Division (Alpine) which was the first alpine division activated in 1943. The division was re-designated as the 10th Mountain Division in 1944 and fought in the mountains of Italy in some of the roughest terrain in World War II. The soldiers of the 10th Mountain Division trained nearby at the former Camp Hale. 10th Mountain Whiskey distills four types of whiskey, plus vodka and liqueur, with tasting rooms and sales at both their Gypsum location and in Vail. Their products are sold at retail outlets in Colorado and Wyoming, as well as California, Georgia and New York.

Philosophy: 10th Mountain actively supports America's military veterans, contributing part of their bottle sales to the Vail Vets Program, the 10th Foundation and War Angel Concerts. More personally, they fervently embrace the mountain lifestyle and honor the 10th Mountain soldiers who inspired a Colorado mountain way of life. In their tasting rooms they proudly display some of the many gifts they have received from active and retired soldiers, and happily share the stories behind them.

Process & Product Notes: Their 86-proof **10th Mountain Rye Whiskey** has a high rye content, yielding a full-bodied and spicy spirit with a touch of toffee. **Colorado Clear Mountain Moonshine** is 80-proof new-make whiskey from 100-percent sweet corn.

ADDRESS
500 Trail Gulch Rd.
Gypsum, Colorado 81637

2ND TASTING ROOM
227 Bridge Street
Vail, Colorado 81657

OWNER(S)
Christian Avignon, Ryan Thompson

CONTACT INFORMATION
Gypsum: 970-524-2580
Vail: 970-470-4215
10thwhiskey.com
facebook.com/10thmtnwhiskey

TASTING ROOM: Yes
TOURS: By appointment

Their **Alpenglow Cordial** is a 70-proof, mixed-grain spirit with notes of peach, vanilla and sage.

Featured Product

For their **10th Mountain Bourbon**—with a mash bill of 75% corn, 21% rye, 4% barley—the grain is milled immediately before cooking to achieve consistent flavor and minimize the chance of degrading bacteria entering the grain. They use a proprietary yeast strain for fermentation, hand cut each distillation, and use a double-distillation process for each batch.

Distillation was begun in August 2013. At that time, they barreled the product in smaller sizes—5, 10, or 30 gallon. Now they age the bourbon in 53-gallon, new white American oak barrels with a level 4 char for at least one year, with older whiskey often included to get the desired flavor profile. Aging takes place in a climate with large temperature fluctuations, which speeds up maturation of the whiskey.

THE SIEBERT SIPPER

Like a Manhattan, but barrel age* it for fully blended, mellow flavor!

- 2 parts 10th Mountain Bourbon
- 1 part Aperol
- 1 part sweet vermouth
- orange peel
- Luxardo cherries

Combine Aperol and sweet vermouth with the Bourbon, pour over ice and garnish with orange peel and a Luxardo cherry.

*Barrel Age: To prep, soak new mini barrel in water overnight. Fill it with your cocktail and age for two weeks. Very special!

Distiller's Tasting Notes: 10th Mountain Bourbon has a nose of medium sweetness with hints of vanilla and oak, plus a touch of honey. The palate is smooth and medium bodied with tastes of toasted nuts. The finish is sweet and medium-long, carrying notes of vanilla.

BRECKENRIDGE DISTILLERY

BRECKENRIDGE DISTILLERY, founded in 2007, is proud to be nestled between peaks of the Continental Divide with its supply of fresh, mineral-rich mountain snowmelt. Known for their award-winning blended straight bourbon whiskey, they also produce malt and specialty whiskeys, gin, rum, vodka and liqueur. They are widely distributed in forty-six states and have two tasting-room locations in Breckenridge. The distillery expanded in 2016 with a New-American Cuisine restaurant and open-air bar.

Philosophy: Breckenridge was established with a commitment to ground a distilled spirits company in the special Colorado high country. As founder Bryan Nolt retells, "Cashing out my life savings, kids' college fund, and eventually selling my house to cover monthly payroll and taxes, we bootstrapped our way through the early years, loving every minute of it." The company spotlights this kind of dedication as an essential value for its ongoing expansion and new products, serving the growing demand for local innovative spirits. "We made it this far by checking our egos at the door, assembling the best cast and crew, and exhibiting the tenacity of a starving honey badger."

Process & Product Notes: Breckenridge places great value on the quality of their high-mountain water because of the "clean, brilliant mouthfeel and smooth finish" it creates in their products. In 2017, they released Aquavit, Peach Bourbon Liquor, Single Barrel Bourbon and Pedro Ximenez Sherry Cask Finish. In January 2018, production facilities were expanded with a new continuous column

ADDRESS
1925 Airport Rd
Breckenridge, Colorado 80424

2ND TASTING ROOM
137 S. Main Street
Breckenridge, Colorado 80424

OWNER(S)
Bryan Nolt

CONTACT INFORMATION
970-547-9759
breckenridgedistillery.com
facebook.com/BreckDistillery

TASTING ROOM: Yes
TOURS: Yes

still for rum and bourbon production.

Breckenridge Dark Arts, a malt whiskey from a barley mash, is processed at lower sugar yields to maximize the flavors of cacao and smoky caramel. Their American-style **Breckenridge Gin** balances the juniper body with notes of bright citrus and spicy undertones achieved through maceration during distillation. The gin carries a delicate floral fragrance that is extracted through a botanical basket during distillation. For the **Breckenridge Spiced Rum,** Turbinado sugars and dark molasses are mashed and distilled in house, aged in casks from their gold medal-winning bourbon, and then finished with roots, spices and dried fruits.

Featured Product

Breckenridge Straight Bourbon Whiskey is a blend of straight bourbons, each aged four to eight years. The blended spirit subsequently is aged in new, char level 3, white American oak in a climate controlled warehouse. For bottling, the bourbon is finished with Breckenridge's mineral-rich snowmelt.

Obi Wan Old Fashioned

- 2-1/2 oz Breckenridge Bourbon—Port Cask Finish
- 2 dashes Breckenridge Barrel Aged Whiskey Bitters
- 1/2 oz Raw Simple Syrup
- Orange peel
- Luxardo cherries

Stir ingredients with ice in a mixing glass. Strain over ice and garnish. Note: Use Blended Straight Bourbon or elevate your classic Old Fashioned by using their Port Cask Finish and Barrel Aged Whiskey Bitters.

Blender's Tasting Notes: This straight bourbon has a deep honey-amber hue with warm, pronounced aromas of underripe banana and brown sugar, with spicy notes of white pepper and toasted sesame. Light body with warm texture and long sweet oak, vanilla finish with a touch of bitterness to balance. Reminiscent of a slice of toasted rye bread with honey drizzled on it.

IDLEWILD SPIRITS & DISTILLERY

IDLEWILD SPIRITS makes bourbon and malt whiskeys, gins, vodkas, rum and liqueur. These are sold at their Winter Park tasting room, featuring a full-service kitchen, and by neighboring liquor stores.

Philosophy: Idlewild Spirits undertakes distilling as a hands-on craft for hand-made quality spirits and innovation. Owner and distiller Jeff Ruhle custom designed the distilling equipment, for example, and they make their ginger beer and tonic water in house. "We don't take shortcuts," Jeff states, "because we want to produce nothing but the best! Some distilleries are in the business because they want to build a brand that they can sell for mega bucks. Fortunately, that is not us. Everyone working here is in it because they love what they do and it really shows in our final product."

Process & Product Notes: Idlewild Spirits **Alpine Gin** is crafted with thirteen different botanicals, where the dominant juniper found in traditional gins is backed down to bring forward more of the other botanical flavors. Jeff reports that "this gin frequently has customers who say they 'are not gin drinkers' take their words back."

Jeff Ruhle is a long-time brewer and, to create their **Colorado Single Malt**, he began with one of his favorite Porter recipes, brewed it without the hops, and ran it through their still. Roasty chocolate, caramel, and coffee notes come through the still bright and clear and, once rested in a barrel, give way to a single-malt whiskey that tastes much older than it is.

ADDRESS
73787 US Hwy 40, Unit 1000
Winter Park, Colorado 80482

OWNER(S)
Jeff Ruhle

CONTACT INFORMATION
970-281-5773
idlewildspirits.com
facebook.com/idlewildspirits

TASTING ROOM: Yes
TOURS: By appointment

For the **Barrel-Aged Coffee Liqueur,** coffee is roasted in house before being cold brewed and mixed with their Rocky Mountain Rum. Left at a strong 60 proof (most coffee liqueurs are 40 proof or less) and lightly sweetened, it is rested in a barrel before being bottled.

Featured Product

Woodcutter's Bourbon is made from Colorado-grown grains that are freshly milled only hours before being combined with pure mountain run-off to start the mashing process.

Every step of the process is controlled to exact specifications for quality. For example, Idlewild invested in more expensive, large conical-bottomed stainless steel fermenters for improved fermentation control. The still also was custom designed to produce a wide variety spirits with exactly the flavor profiles desired.

COLORADO BRAMBLE

- 2 oz Woodcutter's Bourbon
- 1/2 oz Muddled Blackberries
- 1/2 oz freshly squeezed lemon juice
- 1/2 oz Honey Syrup

Add all of the ingredients to a shaker with large ice cubes. Give it 5 or 6 hard shakes, enough to cool the drink and round off the ice cubes. Pour into a rocks glass (including the ice) and top with a lemon zest garnish. — Cereal notes in the whiskey blend incredibly well with the tartness of the fresh blackberries and lemon juice.

Distiller's Tasting Notes: Woodcutter's Bourbon is barrel-aged in high-quality charred new American oak that has been well-seasoned outdoors, lending a smooth and complex tannin profile. The whiskey is aged in both Char 3 and Char 4 barrels and then blended to capture the benefits from both char levels, yielding a whiskey with special complexity that presents an array of cereal notes and is lightly accented by its lengthy rest in the oak.

MARBLE DISTILLING CO.

MARBLE DISTILLING is a craft distillery and boutique luxury inn located in the heart of the Colorado Rocky Mountains and built on a model of sustainability. They make vodka, liqueur, gin and whiskey. The company has two cocktail bars, one at their Carbondale distillery and the other is Marble Bar in Aspen. They distribute products in Colorado and Texas.

Philosophy: Marble Distilling is proud to be a pioneer in sustainable distilling, and their motto—"Drink Sustainably"—speaks mainly to how their spirits are produced. They describe their distillery as a zero-waste facility—perhaps the only one in the world—and adhere to "grain to glass to ground" in-house production methods and commitment to quality.

The majority of their grains are sourced less than one mile from the distillery. Spent mash is returned to local ranches for livestock feed and compost. They recapture all process water and reuse energy from the distillation process to heat their facility, annually saving more than four million gallons of water and 1.8 billion BTUs of energy, enough to heat twenty homes. Their hashtags say it clearly: #LiquidChange #DrinkSustainably.

Process & Product Notes: Pure water and all-natural grains are the cornerstone of their small-batch spirits. Water from the high-mountain Crystal River headwaters are additionally filtered through 99.5 percent calcite Yule marble for all their processes.

Marble Vodka is made with an original blend of all-natural,

ADDRESS
150 Main Street
Carbondale, Colorado 81623

2ND TASTING ROOM
Marble Bar Aspen
415 E. Dean Street
Aspen, Colorado 81611

OWNER(S)
Connie Baker and Wm. Carey Shanks, Michelle Marlow,
Mandy Brennan, Shaefer Welch, Dorian DiPangrazio

CONTACT INFORMATION
Carbondale: 970-963-7008
Aspen: 970-710-2485
marbledistilling.com
facebook.com/MarbleDistilling

TASTING ROOM: Yes
TOURS: By appointment

non-GMO Colorado grains. Soft white wheat and malted barley are distilled five times in a copper pot still for purity and clarity. This is the only vodka filtered through crushed Yule marble, giving it a soft, creamy nose and smooth finish for a distinctive flavor profile. The final distillation is through charred coconut husk via a zero-gravity drip.

Head distiller Connie Baker describes **Moonlight EXpresso** as a modern take on an Old World recipe, as well as a Baker family recipe. Inspired by the Italian craftsmen who worked long hours in the Marble quarry, this complex dark-roasted coffee liqueur blends the sweetness of vanilla bean and natural cane sugar.

Gingercello, also produced in tribute to quarrymen, presents a modern adaptation of the Italian classic. It is made with fresh-cut ginger and the sweetest part of the lemon—hand—zested and left to rest—creating a refreshing taste.

Featured Product

Hoover's Revenge - Ragged Mountain Rye is Marble Distilling's newly released small-batch whiskey. The first release was aged in 30-gallon, new American oak casks with #3 char for 30 months. The spirit is proofed down with marble-filtered water from the Crystal River for bottling at 84 proof.

Distiller's Tasting Notes: Ragged Mountain Rye's mash bill, with rye, wheat and malted barley, affords a smoothness to normally spicy rye. The whiskey is being released in single-cask batches, so each release will have distinctive characteristics.

J.J. CURLEY — "THE NEW OLD FASHIONED"

- 2 oz of Hoover's Revenge
- 1/2 oz Gingercello Reserve
- 3 dashes of bitters
- Ice
- Orange slice
- Cherries

Mix Hoover's Revenge rye whiskey, Gingercello Reserve and bitters. Pour over ice in a rocks glass. Garnish with orange slice and cherry.

PEACH STREET DISTILLERS

PEACH STREET Distillers makes more than twenty-five products, including whiskey, gin, liqueur, vodka and agavé spirits. Their products are distributed in Colorado and Wyoming, plus a growing list of several additional states.

Philosophy: Peach Street prides themselves on innovation and careful execution of small-batch, grain-to-glass craft distilling. "We do it all the hard way, the right way, from the grain to the glass. We experiment. We fail. We get inspired and start experimenting again. There's nothing particularly easy about it. But we've found that hard work tends to pack the best punch, and easy always leaves a bad taste in our mouth."

Process & Product Notes: Peach Street's Pear Brandy and Peach Brandy are both made with local fruit and open-air fermentation.

Each bottle of the **Pear Brandy** is made from twenty pounds of pears and each bottle of **Peach Brandy** from twenty-six pounds of peaches. Both fruits are sourced from local Palisade growers. These brandies are aged in 60-gallon second-use French and American oak barrels. They also make an Apricot Brandy.

Their **Goat Artisan Vodka** has a mash bill of local corn, winter wheat and malted barley. The spirit goes through three distillations and a single charcoal filtration to maintain character and a satisfying flavor.

ADDRESS
144 South Kluge Avenue, Building #2
Palisade, Colorado 81526

OWNER(S)
Bill Graham, David Thibodeau,
Rory Donovan

CONTACT INFORMATION
970-464-1128
peachstreetdistillers.com
facebook.com/PeachStreetDistillers

TASTING ROOM: Yes
TOURS: By appointment

Jackalope Gin begins with hand-picked juniper berries combined with a selection of botanicals, giving the gin a smooth and unconventional flavor that is citrus and slightly nutty.

Featured Product

Peach Street **Colorado Straight Bourbon** is made with sweet western Colorado corn, Colorado rye and pure Rocky Mountain water. The corn is milled and cooked by hand and air fermented.

They distill the mash just once in a Carl brandy pot with a column still. From there it rests in 53-gallon new American white oak barrels for two to five years. Each batch yields just three barrels.

THE HUXLEY

- 1-1/2 oz Peach Street Colorado Straight Bourbon
- 1/2 oz Peach Street Pear or Peach Brandy
- 1/2 oz lime juice
- 1/2 oz sweet vermouth or cherry juice

Serve chilled or pour over ice. Garnish with a cherry.

Distiller's Tasting Notes: The Peach Street Colorado Straight Bourbon aroma has vanilla and cinnamon notes with bold oak character. The first sip is vanilla and corn, followed by more complex cereal and biscuit flavors. Back to vanilla and cinnamon on the finish, which lingers until the next sip. Suggest drinking neat at room temperature.

STEAMBOAT WHISKEY

STEAMBOAT WHISKEY Company, located in Steamboat Springs, is veteran-owned. Their facility also is a pub—licensed to serve alcoholic beverages—unlike most distillery tasting rooms that are licensed only to serve distilled spirits that they make. Steamboat Whiskey follows traditional distilling practices while embracing new trends and experimenting with small-batch recipes and blends.

Their initial product line is distributed in Colorado and includes vodka, gin, blended whiskey and white or new-make whiskey, also known as moonshine. They are working toward producing a full portfolio of whiskeys.

Philosophy: Steamboat Whiskey is dedicated to making high-quality, small-batch spirits by hand, using traditional methods in their American-made pot still. The company grew out of founder Nathan Newhall's passion for the alchemy of distilling and a dream he and his wife, Jessica Newhall, shared to open a distillery in Steamboat Springs, a locale in the Rocky Mountains that they both treasure.

Integral to that dream was the vision of a company in service to the community. They therefore have worked to have a facility where they can share their products and give people a reason to come together and connect with one another. As Nathan observes, "Whiskey is, after all, one of society's oldest social lubricants and has been at the center of social gatherings for millennia. Here at Steamboat Whiskey Company we aim to continue that tradition." More specifically, the company works to support and pay homage to American military veterans.

ADDRESS
55 11th Street
Steamboat Springs, Colorado 80487

OWNER(S)
Nathan Newhall, Jessica Newhall,
Albert Rayle, Megan Rayle

CONTACT INFORMATION
970-846-3534
steamboatwhiskeyco.com
facebook.com/steamboatwhiskey

TASTING ROOM: Yes
TOURS: By appointment

Process & Product Notes: **Ski Town Vodka** is gluten free, made from a mash of corn and potatoes. It is bottled at 88 proof.

Nature's Nectar Honey Spirit starts with a honey mead or wine made from 100-percent mountain wildflower honey. The mead is triple distilled and bottled at 88 proof.

A product in process is their **Sly Eye Rye,** which has a mash bill of 80% rye, 15% corn, 5% malt. It will be bottled at 100 Proof.

Featured Product

Steamboat Whiskey blends their **Warrior Whiskey**, combining two sources—a Rocky Mountain straight bourbon and a Tennessee rye. The bourbon and rye each spend two years in new American oak casks. The blend is finished for three to six months in a Cruzan rum cask and bottled at Navy strength (100 Proof).

Warrior Whiskey is a tribute to American military veterans. Nathan explains that, "A portion of the profits from the sale of Warrior Whiskey goes directly to vetted veteran support organizations so they may continue doing their important work helping soldiers and veterans live the best life possible."

ROLLED FASHIONED

- 2 oz Warrior Whiskey
- 2 dashes sarsaparilla bitters
- 2 dashes Angostura bitters
- 1 mint sprig
- Root beer
- Ice

Combine 100-proof Warrior Whiskey and bitters in shaker. Shake well and strain over ice in Old Fashioned glass. Top with root beer and garnish with mint sprig.

Blender's Tasting Notes: Warrior Whiskey presents a nose with sweet notes of maple syrup, vanilla, Bananas Foster, grilled peaches and white pepper. The palate carries flavors of vanilla, marshmallow, rye spices and raw rope. The finish has light hints of oak, white pepper and cinnamon.

STONEYARD DISTILLERY

STONEYARD
COLORADO SPIRITS

STONEYARD DISTILLERY makes a line of specialty spirits—produced like rum but from Colorado beet sugar—and liqueur. Their products are distributed in Colorado and New Mexico.

Philosophy: Stoneyard conducts their business with a strong sense of independence and self-reliance in building a distillery dedicated to making distinctive spirits from Colorado beet sugar. "There is one thing done here, and that is sugar spirits. Colorado beet sugar, to be exact. To that point, we do what it takes to get the exacting quality that is demanded by operating in the middle of nowhere: Dotsero, Colorado. The result is something that is as unique as Dotsero itself." Max Vogelman, Stoneyard co-owner and head distiller, notes further, " We do everything we can ourselves for the sole purpose of quality and control, and that's the reason we stay local as well."

Process & Product Notes: Stoneyard self-engineered and built their 900-gallon still, and all their products are based on the rum-like "Sugar Spirit" it directly produces. When bottled at 84 proof, they label it Colorado Silver.

Lucky-Oh Horchata Specialty Spirit combines the Sugar Spirit with spices to make a pleasurable Horchata flavor. It is bottled at 70 proof.

Cinnamon Fire combines the Sugar Spirit with organic spicy cinnamon extract, then bottled at 80 proof.

To make **Colorado Coffee Spirit,** the Sugar Spirit is infused with fresh-ground coffee from a local Colorado roaster and bottled at 80 proof.

ADDRESS
4600 Highway 6
Dotsero, Colorado 81637

OWNER(S)
Jim Benson, Max Vogelman

CONTACT INFORMATION
970-471-0284
stoneyarddistillery.com
facebook.com/stoneyarddistillery

TASTING ROOM: Yes
TOURS: Yes

Featured Product

Stoneyard Barrel Reserve is a barrel-aged version of the Sugar Spirit. To make the Sugar Spirit, Colorado beet sugar is fermented in re-purposed dairy tanks and then distilled in small batches in the 900-gallon still that Max Vogelman designed and built from scratch. The product is taken to above 88% alcohol by volume (ABV) at the still, then barreled at 60% ABV in 53-gallon second-use bourbon barrels for at least two years. It is bottled at 40% ABV (80 proof) for the Barrel Reserve.

The ingredients and processing create a "specialty spirit" that has no classical category—which means, happily for the Stoneyard team, that they can develop custom methods in distilling and finishing products to achieve their own goals for unique flavors and distinctive quality.

SPIRITINI

- 3 oz Stoneyard Barrel Reserve
- 1/2 oz dry vermouth
- Ice

For a unique take on the martini form, add Barrel Reserve and vermouth to a shaker with ice. Stir or shake. Pour and add your favorite garnish.

Distiller's Tasting Notes: Stoneyard Barrel Reserve presents a very sweet nose with a light but distinct woodiness. Light and airy in the mouth, it carries some pleasant heat on the tongue, with slight caramel flavor and a nice earthiness. With oak present throughout, the finish is dry and complex.

WOODY CREEK DISTILLERS

WOODY CREEK Distillers products include bourbon, malt and rye whiskeys, gin, rum and vodka. Their spirits are distributed in Colorado, New Mexico and at least sixteen more states across the country.

Philosophy: Woody Creek Distillers was founded to build a lasting legacy for their families and their community by making the finest craft spirits, each with a unique taste and character true to the origins of that spirit. Grounded in a farming region, they are proud to use produce grown on their own family farm and the farms of their neighbors. They are dedicated to protecting and enhancing the natural resources of Woody Creek. The distillery is a low-emissions facility, using the most efficient distillation technology available, and waste from raw products goes back to the family farm in Woody Creek as compost or to local ranches as livestock feed.

Process & Product Notes: Woody Creek distills all their spirits in house with custom Carl stills. They source their grains only from trusted Colorado farms, and they grow and harvest some of their own ingredients.

Their gluten-free **Potato Vodka**, distilled from potatoes they grow themselves in the Roaring Fork Valley, won Double Gold and Best Vodka at the San Francisco World Spirits Competition.

Woody Creek Bourbon is mashed, fermented and distilled from 100-percent Colorado-grown corn, rye, wheat and barley, then aged for at least four years.

ADDRESS
60 Sunset Dr
Basalt, Colorado 81621

OWNER(S)
Mary Scanlan, Pat Scanlan,
Mark Kleckner

CONTACT INFORMATION
970-279-5110
woodycreekdistillers.com
facebook.com/WoodyCreekDistillers

TASTING ROOM: Yes
TOURS: By appointment

Woody Creek Gin combines classic London Dry and New World styles. They start with their Potato Vodka and distill it to above 190 proof.

Locally-sourced, hand-picked juniper berries are mixed with other botanicals, such as fresh lemongrass, coriander, cinnamon, angelica, hibiscus, lavender, cranberries and grains of paradise, as well as fresh orange and lemon peel and lime wedge. The base spirit and the botanicals are left to macerate for a full day at 150 degrees Fahrenheit and then re-distilled, resulting in a very smooth American gin with great complexity and character.

Featured Product

Woody Creek Straight Rye Whiskey is made from 100-percent Colorado rye with a distinct and complex rye character. The spirit is mashed, fermented, distilled and barrel aged on site. Head distiller David Matthews matures the whiskey at least two years in 53-gallon charred new American white oak barrels. It is bottled at 90 proof.

THE BOZ

- 2 oz Straight Rye Whiskey
- 1/2 oz lemon juice
- 1/2 oz simple syrup
- Fresh basil
- Fresh ginger
- Raspberries

Shake liquid ingredients vigorously in tin. Double strain over ice with basil raspberry garnish. To make garnish, muddle basil, fresh ginger and raspberries.

Distiller's Tasting Notes: Woody Creek Straight Rye Whiskey presents flavors of rye bread and dried orchard fruit on the entry followed by spice, cinnamon and clove. Tastes of rye grain and roasted almond carry through mid-palate. The long finish has resurgent baking spice notes. Winner of double gold medal at San Francisco World Spirits Competition.

COLORADO: SOUTHWEST AREA

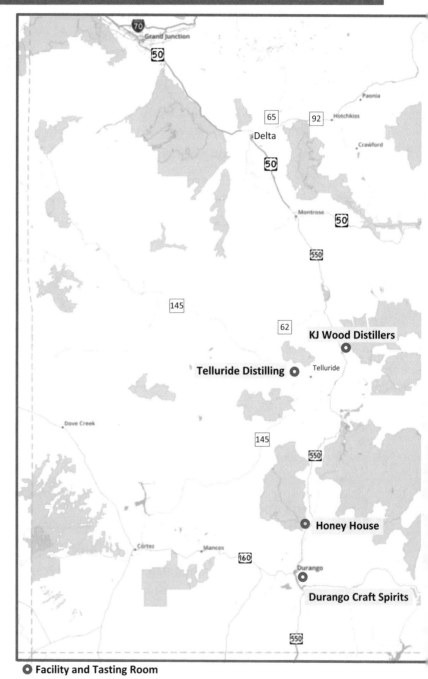

70
Grand Junction
50

65   92   Paonia
Hotchkiss
Delta
50   Crawford

Montrose
50

550

145

62
KJ Wood Distillers

Telluride Distilling   Telluride

Dove Creek

145
550

Honey House

Cortez   Mancos

160
Durango

Durango Craft Spirits

550

⊙ Facility and Tasting Room

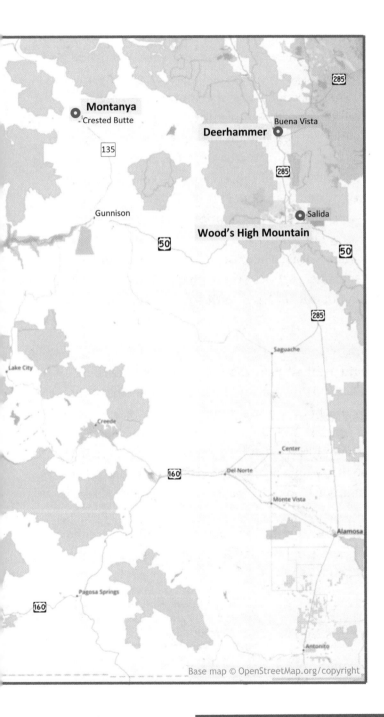

DEERHAMMER

DEERHAMMER IS a family-owned, small-batch distillery, founded in 2010. They make malt whiskey and gin, with a bourbon and a rye whiskey in process. Limited release or distillery-only spirits also are produced. Their products are distributed in Colorado.

Philosophy: While grounded in traditional whiskey-making, especially Scotch whiskey, Deerhammer is dedicated to innovation and discovery in making fine spirits that express their origin in the Colorado high mountain valley of the Arkansas River. As Lenny Eckstein, head distiller and co-founder, states: "At Deerhammer, our distilling is steeped in whiskey tradition, but our methods are infused with curiosity and creativity."

Process & Product Notes: Their **Dutch Style Gin** is made with all malted barley, a traditional Genever with gentle pine flavor. It is infused with fifteen botanicals after distillation, giving the gin a nuanced flavor profile.

Featured Product

American Single Malt Whiskey is Deerhammer's "corner-stone" product, handmade by feel and taste from a porter-style, 100-percent barley mash that melds complexities from four varieties of kilned and roasted barley.

For enhanced flavors, the mash ferments over four days in the open air using a heritage American bourbon yeast strain. Natural flora in the mountain air shape the mash, capturing distinct influences from the Colorado terroir.

The whiskey is double distilled in copper pot stills fashioned after traditional designs from Scotland. Although less efficient than

ADDRESS
321 East Main Street
Buena Vista, Colorado 81211

OWNER(S)
Lenny Eckstein, Amy Eckstein

CONTACT INFORMATION
719-395-9464
deerhammer.com
facebook.com/deerhammer

TASTING ROOM: Yes
TOURS: Yes

commonly-used column stills, the pot stills are employed to achieve complexity of flavor and unusually long finish.

The spirit is heated with direct fire, a rarely-used traditional method, to contribute rich toasted caramel notes to the whiskey. Distilling at 8,000 feet elevation also benefits the process, allowing the pot stills to run cooler than at sea level, which maintains more unique flavors from the grain bill.

The malt whiskey ages for at least two years in 53-gallon, new American oak barrels, heavy toast, #2 char. Each cask comes of age at a different time, determined by frequent tasting, not a prescribed age statement. High- and low-pressure systems that move through the high-altitude environment expedite the whiskey maturation, as do drastic temperature swings (from 40°F to 80°F in a day) that accelerate the interaction of whiskey and wood, imparting intensified flavor notes and complexity.

TROUT'S TAIL

- 1-1/2 oz American Single Malt Whiskey
- 3/4 oz allspice dram
- 1/2 oz lime juice
- 1/4 oz simple syrup
- 2 dashes Angostura bitters

Combine Deerhammer American Single Malt and other ingredients. Shake with ice and strain into a chilled coupe.

Distiller's Tasting Notes: Bottled at 92 proof, American Single Malt has a complex profile and bold, rich flavor. It presents aromas of peanut brittle, roasted cacao, caramel and oatmeal. The malt flavors carry tastes of dark chocolate, coffee, graham cracker, vanilla and tobacco. With a medium to full body, it has a dry, yet fruity finish with hazelnut and chocolate.

DURANGO CRAFT SPIRITS

URANGO CRAFT Spirits began distilling in December 2014 and is Durango's first grain-to-glass distillery since Prohibition. Their spirits are hand crafted, mashed, distilled and bottled in their distillery in downtown Durango. They currently make a white whiskey, bourbon and vodka. Their products are distributed in Colorado.

Philosophy: The distillery's products use all Colorado ingredients, and they enjoy sharing stories of Durango's past through their spirits and cocktails. Each of their bottles shares a tale that highlights the settlers who were important in the founding of Durango in 1881.

Process & Product Notes: Durango Craft Spirits uses non-GMO white corn from the Ute Mountain Ute Tribe and grains that are all Colorado from the Colorado Malting Company in Alamosa, Colorado.

Soiled Doves Vodka, bottled at 80 proof, pays homage to Durango's frontier ladies of the night. As Michael McCardell has pointed out, "one must not overlook the role the brothels of the Red Light District played in its establishment. Prostitution was a prospering industry and, due to its seamy nature, gave rise to the euphemism Soiled Doves. At the turn of the 20th century, brothels thrived between Main Avenue and the Animas River to the west.

"The fines accrued from the brothels, as well as the business drawn from nearby towns, provided the income necessary for the budding city to build its first schools and police department. The

ADDRESS
1120 Main Avenue, Suite 2
Durango, Colorado 81301

OWNER(S)
Michael McCardell, Amy McCardell

CONTACT INFORMATION
970-247-1919
durangospirits.com
facebook.com/durangospirits

TASTING ROOM: Yes
TOURS: By appointment

gains provided by Soiled Doves, despite their igno-
minious trade, entrenched the roots of a town that
has blossomed into the community Durango is
today."

Mayday Moonshine, bottled at 90 proof, is
named after Mayday Mine which lies in the La Plata
mountains just west of Durango. Prohibition was
passed in Colorado in 1916 (four years before the
rest of the country) and at the same time the
silver market crashed, causing many mines to
close. Moonshiners subsequently hid their stills in
abandoned mines and made moonshine under their
cover.

Featured Product

Cinder Dick Straight Bourbon was released in
December 2017 after being aged in new American oak charred barrels for more than two
years. It is 94 proof and made from corn,
wheat, rye, barley and malted barley. Cinder
Dick honors the days of the railroad and the men and women who
helped build Durango.

Distiller's Tasting Notes: This product has the traditional
notes of fine bourbon with vanilla and caramel up front, and a surprising note of banana on the finish.

THE PORTER

- 1-1/2 oz Cinder Dick Bourbon
- 1 Demerara sugar cube
- 3 dashes Angostura bitters
- 1 large ice sphere
- 1 Bada Bing cherry
- 1 fresh orange slice

Muddle a Demerara Sugar Cube with the bitters and a splash of water.
Pace in rocks glass with ice. Stir in Cinder Dick Bourbon and garnish with
cherry and orange slice.

HONEY HOUSE DISTILLERY

HONEY HOUSE Distillery is owned and operated from a fourth-generation family beekeeping business called Honeyville. They produce honey-infused bourbon whiskeys, rum, vodka and liqueur. Their products are sold in Colorado and Wyoming, and will soon be sold in New Mexico and Texas.

Philosophy: Honey House Distillery was started in 2012 to create unique spirits that include their Mountain Wildflower Honey. Founders Adam Bergal and Kevin Culhane are proud to be extending the legacy of Kevin's grandfather, Vern Culhane, whose passion for beekeeping and honey launched the Honeyville business in 1918.

Kevin's parents grew the business, specializing in small-batch, hand-crafted honeys, syrups, jams and sauces. In their turn, Adam and Kevin are dedicated to creating small-batch, hand-crafted honey spirits.

Process & Product Notes: For their **Hex Vodka**, Honey House creates a mead by fermenting their Wildflower Honey and distilling the mead to create a vodka that's finally blended with another grain vodka. The result is a non-sweet vodka with subtle wildflower notes.

The Honey House **Red Cliffs Spiced Rum** is distilled from a traditional molasses and brown sugar blend for a flavorful white rum. The rum next is placed in used whiskey barrels and infused

ADDRESS
33633 Hwy 550
Durango, Colorado 81301

OWNER(S)
Adam Bergal, Kevin Culhane

CONTACT INFORMATION
970-247-1474
honeyhousedistillery.com
facebook.com/honeyhousedistillery

TASTING ROOM: Yes
TOURS: No

with fresh ground spices and blended with caramelized honey for sweetness and a smoky finish.

Release of another product, **Durango Joe's Liqueur**, is pending.

Featured Product

To blend their **Colorado Honey Whiskey**, Honey House combines 5-year and 7-year bourbons with their own Mountain Wildflower Honey. After blending, the spirit is twice polished.

Blender's Tasting Notes: The select, aged bourbons and the Wildflower Honey blend in Colorado Honey Whiskey to create a subtly sweet, smoky honey bourbon whiskey.

Stinger

- 2 oz Colorado Honey Whiskey
- 1-1/2 oz chokecherry lime mixer
- Large ice cubes
- Club soda

Stir Honey Whiskey with chokecherry lime mixer in a highball glass with ice. Top with club soda.

K J Wood Distillers

K J Wood Distillers products include bourbon and rye whiskeys, gin and vodka, which they distribute in Colorado.

Philosophy: KJ Wood Distillers approaches craft distilling as an artform. They also honor the long heritage of distilling and are building their business to be a legacy for their family and the community. The ethos of K J Wood Distillers is to serve both through "a truly hand-crafted spirit that reflects the values of Colorado and the southwestern United States."

Emblematic of this sense of heritage, their stills were named after family members of founder and owner K John Wood: "Big Larry, our mash tank/ wash still is named for K John's late father-in-law, a true patron of whiskey. Tommy, our spirit still, is named after great-grand father, who owned a pub in the family's native land of England. And Libby, our Jinn* still, named for Granny; who always had two fingers of gin before bedtime. (*Because to those who grew up in the old Raj period of Mesopotamia, Jinn gin was Ohh so comforting!)"

Process & Product Notes: Located in Ouray at 8500 feet elevation, KJ Wood Distillers bases its craft spirits on the cornerstone of great water, utilizing crystal waters of the Rocky Mountain high country, together with fine ingredients—from locally-sourced barley and blue corn, to select European juniper berries, to premium spices from the Orient.

Ourye Whiskey, named in wordplay with its birthplace of Ouray, this 100-percent rye mash whiskey is aged for one year in new American oak casks. Its heritage spirit is a Ute proverb:

ADDRESS
929 Main Street
Ouray, Colorado 81427

OWNER(S)
K John Wood

CONTACT INFORMATION
970-325-7295
kjwooddistillers.com
facebook.com/KJWoodDistillersInc

TASTING ROOM: Yes
TOURS: By appointment

"Don't walk behind me; I may not lead. Don't walk in front of me; I may not follow. Walk beside me that we may be as one."

Berthoud Blue Vodka is distilled with blue corn for a distinctive vodka. It is named in homage to the Wood family's roots in Berthoud, Colorado.

Their **Dead Drift Bourbon** is distilled with special regard for the mountain water, and they utilize local blue corn and other grains for the mash.

Featured Product

Jinn Gin was first produced in 2013 and soon won a gold medal at the New York World Wine and Spirits Competition. Production of the gin begins with a corn-based grain neutral spirit (GNS) and a solution of thirteen botanicals— including lavender flowers, hops flowers, lemon and orange zest—that are macerated in a kettle for twenty-four hours.

The neutral spirit is re-distilled in a single pot still with the solution of botanicals and bottled in house after blending with water to 80 proof.

WHO YOU CALLING OLD FASHIONED?

- 2 oz Dead Drift or Ourye Whiskey
- 1 sugar cube
- 3 dashes Angostura Bitters
- 1 dash orange bitters
- 1 ice sphere

Mix ingredients and pour over ice. Garnish with an orange expression.
Option: Use Demerara or Turbinado syrup instead of sugar cube.

Montanya Distillers

MONTANYA DISTILLERS produces rum and cocktail bitters. Founded in 2008, they are among the pioneers of the Colorado distilling industry. Their products are distributed in Colorado and 41 other states, plus most European Union countries.

Philosophy: "Our vision as a company," states co-owner Karen Hoskin, "is to be the most highly-respected and well-loved American rum available. We intend to stay true to our craft distilling values as we grow. We are also changing how Americans view rum cocktails by introducing new artisan cocktails in our tasting rooms every week, all year round." This commitment is paired with adoption of the most sustainable environmental practices in the world throughout their business, from 100-percent wind power to zero-waste campaigns in distillery and tasting room. More than two dozen programs are detailed on their website.

Process & Product Notes: Distilled from American sugar cane, **Montanya Platino** ages for one year in second-use Colorado whiskey barrels and is filtered through a coconut husk charcoal filter to remove color. Platino has the smoothness and complex flavors of an aged rum, without cloying sweetness. A touch of Colorado mountain honey added at bottling brings out natural barrel and rum flavors. Prominent flavors include biscotti, cream soda, cardamom, coffee, vanilla and black pepper. It has received nine gold medals and two "Best in Class" designations in international competitions, as well as "Best White Rum" at the World Rum Awards, UK 2015.

Montanya Exclusiva is a limited release currently available only in Colorado. It is barrel aged for two years in second-use

ADDRESS
212 Elk Avenue
Crested Butte, Colorado 81224

OWNER(S)
Karen Hoskin, Brice Hoskin

CONTACT INFORMATION
970-799-3206
montanyadistillers.com
facebook.com/MontanyaDistillers

TASTING ROOM: Yes
TOURS: Yes

Colorado whiskey barrels and six more months in used wine barrels. The rum is smooth, with a dry, tannin finish rare in aged rums. The flavor profile is deeply complex with cinnamon, red wine, honey and vanilla flavors, without overwhelming sweetness.

Montanya also crafts perhaps the only rum-based flavor-infused **Cocktail Bitters** in the world. They may be ordered directly on the Montanya website.

Featured Product

Montanya Oro is a dark aged rum distilled from Louisiana sugar cane that is fermented in 250-gallon batches over about seven days. Montanya uses custom alembic copper pot stills with double reflux. The spirit is aged one year or longer in second-use select Colorado whiskey barrels for fuller body and oak flavors. Temperatures fluctuate twenty to thirty degrees daily in the barrel room, which intensifies the rum's exposure to the wood and its benefits.

At bottling, the Oro receives a touch of honey gathered from nearby hives. Never filtered, the rum retains natural color from the barrel along with a slight tint from the caramelized honey. No molasses caramel, artificial coloring or flavoring are used. Some longer-aged batches of Oro are finished in French oak that previously held port.

MONTANYA OLD FASHIONED

- 3 oz Montanya Oro rum
- 5 drops Montanya Citrus Bitters
- 1/4 oz simple syrup
- 1 pinch sugar
- 1 ice sphere
- 1 fresh orange slice
- 2 Amarena or Luxardo cherries

In rocks glass, muddle together orange slice, one cherry and a pinch of sugar. Add syrup, rum and bitters, plus ice. Stir (do not shake) until chilled. Garnish with remaining cherry.

Distiller's Tasting Notes: Flavors prominent in the Oro include red chili, coffee, caramel, vanilla, pineapple and chocolate. The Oro has received eight silver medals and one "Best In Class" designation in competitions.

TELLURIDE DISTILLING

Telluride Distilling continues the whiskey-making tradition of their high-mountain town, from its storied moonshining history throughout Prohibition to today, beginning distillation of their whiskey in 2014 as Telluride's first legal distillery. They make whiskey, vodka and liqueur, which are distributed in Colorado.

Philosophy: Owner Abbott Smith and his compadres at Telluride Distilling approach both their business and enjoying whiskey as adventures. They build their own equipment, hand-process their ingredients and strive to make distinctly memorable spirits.

Process & Product Notes: Telluride Distilling's in-house processes include hand mashing and mixing in their own handmade 300-gallon mash tun, controlled environment fermentation in 550-gallon stainless steel tanks, and distillation in their custom-built continuous fractionating column still. All products are produced and proofed with pure water from Telluride Mountain.

Telluride Vodka is made from 100-percent cane sugar with twenty-six "theoretical" distillations in the continuous fractionating column still. The spirit then passes through a multi-stage filtration process. Bottled at 80 proof, the gluten-free vodka has a smooth, creamy mouthfeel.

Based on a recipe in the European Alps style, **Chairlift Warmer Peppermint Schnapps** is sweet, without being syrupy, with a peppermint flavor. It was the first peppermint schnapps to win a gold

ADDRESS
152B Society Drive
Telluride, Colorado 81435

OWNER(S)
Abbott Smith

CONTACT INFORMATION
970-239-6052
telluridedistilling.com
facebook.com/telluridedistillingcompany

TASTING ROOM: Yes
TOURS: Yes

medal at the San Francisco World Spirits Competition. Bottled at 100 proof, it is a gluten-free product.

Telluride Aromatic Bitters is a cane spirit aged in fifteen different herbs and spices for thirty days before going through an intense filtering process to eliminate unpalatable oils. It's a flavorful additive for a savory lift to your cocktails.

Featured Product

Head distiller Abbott Smith makes **Telluride Whiskey** in a continuous fractionating column still from a 100-percent malted barley mash. Aged first in new 53-gallon charred oak barrels for at least two years, the whiskey then undergoes finishing for additional flavoring in a variety of used casks—red wine, port and sherry, among others—for at least six more months. It is bottled at 92 proof.

Telluride Flatliner

A cult favorite served everywhere in Telluride.

- 2 parts Telluride Vodka
- 1 part Chairlift Warmer Peppermint Schnapps
- 1 part chilled espresso
- 1 part half-and-half cream
- 1 part Monin vanilla syrup

Just mix. Cold brew espresso is a good alternative to chilled espresso.

Distiller's Tasting Notes: Quality ingredients, pure mountain water, hands-on processing, precise distillation with the custom-designed still, and aging on new oak with extended special cask finishing—together these create a whiskey with great depth and complexity. It has a light body and warm texture, with hints of vanilla, honey and chocolate.

WOOD'S HIGH MOUNTAIN DISTILLERY

Wood's High Mountain Distillery, founded by brothers P.T. and Lee Wood, makes malt and rye whiskey, gin, vodka and liqueur. Their products are distributed in Colorado, California, New Jersey, New York and in the European Union.

Philosophy: Wood's High Mountain Distillery is the realization of a dream that P.T. Wood brought home from an extended rafting trip through the Grand Canyon. After many days on the river, and many bottles of whiskey shared among friends, the inspiration to distill spirits was born.

Following years of planning, happenstance and labor, the Wood brothers opened the distillery in 2012 "with the goal to bottle our passion for outdoor adventures with spirits that shine with the essence of the mountains of Colorado." With that purpose, they pride themselves on distilling small-batch spirits, from grain to glass, using the freshest, local ingredients available.

Process & Product Notes: Made with spicy rye malt and specialty barley malts, their **Alpine Rye Whiskey** has a flavor profile of smoky rye spice, cinnamon, caramel, orange peel and coffee. It is aged for two years in new oak barrels. Bottled in limited release batches, it is available only a few times a year.

Treeline Gin is a Colorado modern gin with a botanical selection inspired by traditional London dry gins. Distilled from grain spirits with Colorado-grown Rocky Mountain juniper, it has flavors of juniper and hints of citrus, licorice and pepper notes.

ADDRESS
144 W 1st Street
Salida, Colorado 81201
OWNER(S)
P.T. Wood, Lee Wood

CONTACT INFORMATION
719-207-4315
woodsdistillery.com
facebook.com/woodsdistillery

TASTING ROOM: Yes
TOURS: Yes

Mountain Hopped Gin offers an alternative botanical mix, featuring Rocky Mountain juniper, Colorado-grown Cascade hops, elderflowers and selected spices. The gin has an earthy flavor, with floral and citrus forward notes and a hint of sweetness.

Featured Product

Wood's **Tenderfoot Malt Whiskey** is created with a blend of malted grains, including two-row malted barley, chocolate malted barley, cherrywood-smoked malted barley, malted rye and malted wheat. It is aged in new American white oak barrels and bottled at 90 proof.

PT's First Street Cocktail

- 1-1/2 oz Tenderfoot Single Malt Whiskey
- 1/2 oz Fleur de Sureau Elderflower Liqueur
- 2 dashes bitters

Stir over ice and strain into coupe, served neat.

Distiller's Tasting Notes: Tenderfoot Malt Whiskey has a pale amber color and bright aromas of raisin bran, dried peach and suede. It has a zesty, medium-to-full body that is dry, yet fruity, with a warming rye character. The finish is of medium length, sweet with peppery spices, nuts, charcoals and rye flour tones.

New Mexico

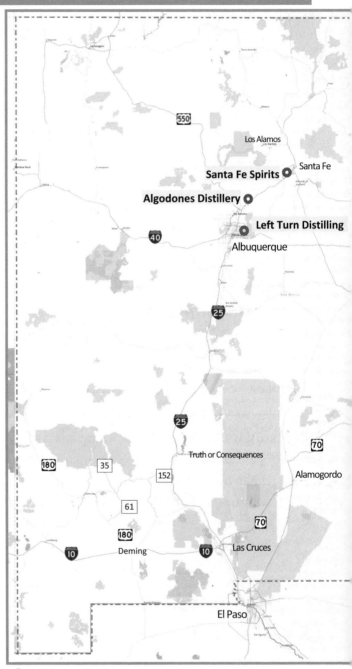

● **Facility and Tasting Room**

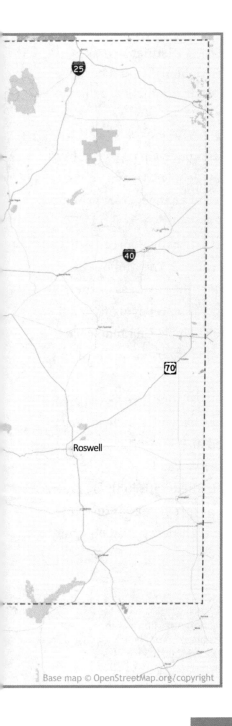

Base map © OpenStreetMap.org/copyright

ALGODONES DISTILLERY

ALGODONES DISTILLERY—THE Arts & Crafts Distillery—makes gin, vodka, white whiskey and liqueur, with bourbon and corn whiskey scheduled for release in 2018. Their products are distributed in New Mexico.

Philosophy: Algodones Distillery embraces the Arts & Crafts Movement philosophy that something handmade enriches the lives of those it touches and influences the way people live and relate to the outside world. They feel that in times of change, craft grounds and humanizes us.

Their guiding tenet is "Small Batched + Locally Sourced + Kindly Crafted - For the Spirit of New Mexico." They follow that ethos in making distilled spirits that reflect the richness of their high-desert bosque agriculture, water and climate, by using traditional pot stills, locally sourced ingredients (including blue corn, piñon and juniper), artesian well water, and their bosque location for aging.

Process & Product Notes: **Claro "Clear Diamond" Vodka** is a corn spirit that is distilled five times and then filtered for a clean, crisp taste with a slightly sweet finish. Bottled at 80 proof, it won a gold medal at the 2016 American Craft Spirits Awards.

Ginebra Southwestern Dry Gin is distilled with juniper, lavender, piñon, prickly pear, rose petals and desert sage to infuse this contemporary gin with essences of these high-desert and bosque botanicals.

ADDRESS
15 Calle Alfredo
Algodones, New Mexico 87001

OWNER(S)
Gregory R. McAllister, Peter D. Pacheco

CONTACT INFORMATION
505-301-9992
Algodonesdistillery.com
facebook.com/Algodones-Distillery-478739985561539

TASTING ROOM: Yes
TOURS: By appointment

Their Ginebra Southwestern could be classed as a "New Western Dry Gin," which are gins that move away from the usually dominant focus on juniper to other botanicals, often regionally grown, that share the flavor stage in a balanced way with the juniper. The Ginebra Southwestern is bottled at 80 proof.

Enebro Juniper Liqueur starts with their Ginebra recipe and takes it back toward a London Dry by adding more juniper ("enebro"), but also more lavender and then sweetened. It is bottled at 75 proof.

Featured Product

Head distiller Greg McAllister makes **Luna Blue Corn Moonshine** with a mash of 80% corn and 20% malted barley, using native-grown, roasted New Mexico blue corn. Crafted unaged as white whiskey suitable for sipping, Luna also forms the foundation for their forthcoming aged corn whiskey and young bourbon.

Distiller's Tasting Notes: New Mexico blue corn, noted for its nutty and sweet profile, imparts to Luna Blue Corn Moonshine tastes of roasted corn and nuts, with a sweet finish, for a distinctive taste of the Southwest.

SANDIA MARTINI

Sandia means "watermelon" in Spanish. This recipe pays homage to local mountain sunset hues.

- 1-1/2 oz Claro "Clear Diamond" Vodka
- 3 oz fresh watermelon juice
- 1 lime wedge
- simple syrup, to taste

Combine Claro Vodka, fresh squeezed and strained watermelon juice, and simple syrup (to taste) in a cocktail shaker and mix vigorously. Strain into chilled martini glass (option: rim with sugar). Garnish with lime and serve.

LEFT TURN DISTILLING

L EFT TURN Distilling, Albuquerque's first distillery, makes corn whiskey, gin, rum, vodka and liqueur, with malt whiskey and brandy as works in process. Their products are distributed in New Mexico and pending for Colorado.

Philosophy: Left Turn Distilling is committed to hand crafting their spirits. This extends to their stills and other equipment. Founder and distiller Brian Langwell began distilling with a chemistry set at the age of fifteen. Years later, in 2013, Brian sold his machine shop and began Left Turn Distilling, which included building all the stills, tank and process equipment. "All of our spirits," he explains, "are hand distilled with only the finest raw ingredients and purest water. We take pride in all of our uniquely Southwest products."

Process & Product Notes: Left Turn Distilling presents **Rojo Piñon Rum** as "the world's first piñon-flavored rum." It is a traditional Carribean-style rum made from molasses, but with a southwest twist—Piloncillo sugar is added to the mash for flavor.

After fermenting, the rum is distilled in their handmade pot still, then finished with oak chips and roasted New Mexico piñon nuts added for a robust nutty flavor.

Their **La Luz Vodka,** as its name suggests, is a smooth, very light tasting spirit for cocktails without the taste of vodka.

Brothers Old Tom Gin is made in a style common before Prohibition, based on a recipe popular in 18th-century England. Slightly sweeter with more accessible flavors than London Dry, but drier than the predecessor, Genever, Old Tom* gin sometimes is called

ADDRESS
2924 Girard Boulevard NE
Albuquerque, New Mexico 87107

OWNER(S)
Brian Langwell, Robert Palmer

CONTACT INFORMATION
505-508-0508
leftturndistilling.com
facebook.com/leftturndistilling

TASTING ROOM: Yes
TOURS: By appointment

"The Missing Link." Brothers Old Tom Gin is dry-infused to achieve a gentle flavor balance. Bottled at 90 proof, the gin is slightly sweet with light juniper and distinct citrus flavors.

* The name Old Tom Gin purportedly came from wooden plaques shaped like a black cat—an "old tom"— mounted on the outside wall of a pub in 18th-century England. After a pedestrian deposited a penny in the cat's mouth, they would place their lips around a small tube between the cat's paws. From the tube would come a shot of gin, poured by the bartender inside the pub.

Featured Product

New Mexico Blue Corn Whiskey is made with 100-percent blue corn from local New Mexico sources. The corn is roasted and ground, then triple distilled in a traditional manner in their copper artisan pot still. The whiskey is lightly aged in used bourbon barrels and finished with oak chips to preserve the corn flavor characteristics of traditional corn whiskey.

AUTUMN OLD FASHIONED

A classic cocktail with the flavor of Fall.

- 2 oz New Mexico Blue Corn Whiskey
- 1/4 oz simple syrup
- 3 dashes black walnut bitters

- 1 large ice sphere
- 1 orange twist
- 1 Luxardo cherry

Stir Blue Corn Whiskey, syrup and bitters in a rocks glass with large ice cubes or sphere. Garnish with orange twist and cherry.

Distiller's Tasting Notes: New Mexico Blue Corn Whiskey is a robust, full-bodied whiskey. It has traditional distinct corn flavors, with subtle notes of buttered popcorn, a very light oak character and a mild chocolate finish.

SANTA FE SPIRITS

SANTA FE Spirits makes malt whiskey, gin, vodka and liqueur. Their products are distributed in Colorado and New Mexico, as well as Georgia, Idaho, Illinois, Montana, Nevada, New York, Oregon, Texas and Wisconsin.

Philosophy: Santa Fe Spirits was founded by Colin Keegan in 2010 with the goal of becoming the Southwest's pre-eminent artisan distillery. Colin admits that, as an Englishman, he carries a long-established appreciation of good Scotch, but he is not interested in mimicking "peat-smoked whiskeys." "Our goal," he emphasizes, "is to produce exceptional spirits designed to capture and accentuate the essence of the Southwest."

Process & Product Notes: Wheeler's Western Dry Gin is the fruition after two years of work hand-collecting native southwestern botanicals and perfecting the recipe to create a classic dry gin with Southwestern flair. The distillery utilizes both maceration and vapor extraction as suited for each botanical—including cholla cactus blossom, desert sage, juniper, osha root and hops—to capture its fullest expression in the gin.

With **Silver Coyote Pure Malt Whiskey**, Santa Fe Spirits makes an unaged spirit reminiscent of the pure-malt whiskies produced in the UK, rather than a corn-based white-dog whiskey. A combination of Scottish yeast, European and American malts, and traditional distilling techniques produces a subtle spirit expressing hints of fruit aromatics, followed by a smooth mouthfeel with sweet,

ADDRESS
7505 Mallard Way, Unit i
Santa Fe, New Mexico 87507

2ND TASTING ROOM
308 Read Street
Santa Fe, New Mexico 87501

OWNER(S)
Colin Keegan

CONTACT INFORMATION
Distillery: 505-467-8892
Tasting Room: 505-780-5906
santafespirits.com
facebook.com/santafespirits

TASTING ROOM: Yes
TOURS: Yes

malty notes and a dry, earthy finish. Bottled at 92 proof.

For their **Atapiño Liqueur**, piñon nuts are roasted and soaked in a barrel with Silver Coyote whiskey for two months. Next the spirit is sweetened with hand-collected ponderosa pine resin and sugar to produce a liqueur with the essence of piñon. It is a seasonal, limited release; only in 375 milliliter bottles.

Featured Product

Colkegan Single Malt Whiskey is a Scottish-style whiskey from 100% malted barley, but with key differences. The mash bill includes 30% mesquite-smoked barley, used by no other distillery. Through a unique process, the whiskey matures in approximately 30% new oak barrels and 70% used bourbon barrels for color and sweetness; they are held in a climate-controlled barrel warehouse—with a specific temperature regimen ranging from freezing to swelteringly hot, and humidity from bone dry to extremely damp—to further enhance complexity in the spirit. Current batches are aged at least 3-1/2 years.

Smoky Manhattan

Smoky and sweet, it's a treat.

- 3 oz Colkegan Single Malt Whiskey
- 1 oz sweet vermouth
- 3 shakes Angostura bitters
- 1 cherry

Stir Colkegan, sweet vermouth and bitters in a pint glass. Never shake. Strain into a martini glass and garnish with cherry.

Distiller's Tasting Notes: Colkegan has a nose that's malty, with distinct grainy notes, sweet honey and apricots, and smoky toasted oak. The palate has tastes of fresh ground coffee, dark bitter chocolate, cigar boxes, smoke and vanilla. It is rich on the front of the palate with a spicy finish.

WYOMING

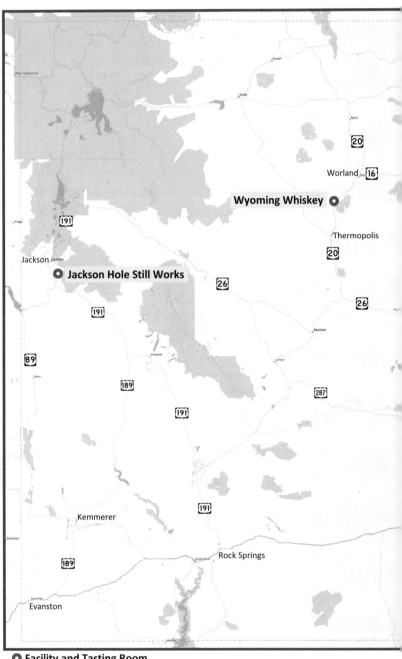

Worland [16]

[20]

Wyoming Whiskey ⊙

Thermopolis

[20]

[191]

Jackson

⊙ **Jackson Hole Still Works**

[26]

[26]

[191]

[89]

[189]

[287]

[191]

[191]

Kemmerer

Rock Springs

[189]

Evanston

⊙ **Facility and Tasting Room**

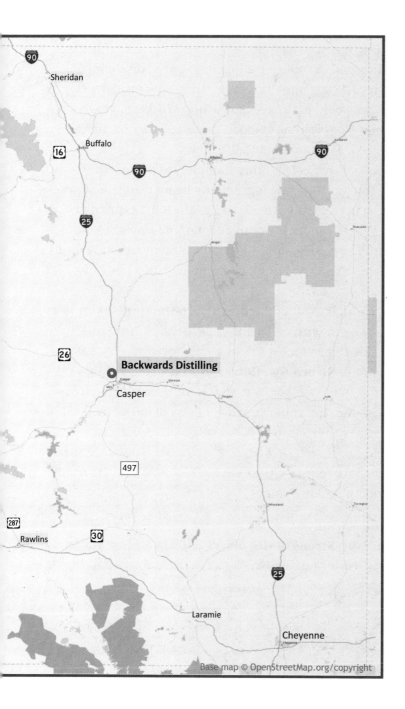

BACKWARDS DISTILLING CO.

BACKWARDS DISTILLING was founded by the Pollock family in 2013 with the goal of building a business based on their passion for food, cocktails and craft beer. They now produce eight types of spirits: bourbon, malt, rye and white whiskeys, gin, rum, vodka and liqueur. Their circus-themed products are distributed in Wyoming, Colorado, Montana and California.

Philosophy: Backwards Distilling Company is dedicated to creating authentic spirits from raw ingredients using traditional practices. "Each spirit is created with cocktails in mind," explains head distiller Chad Pollock, "and we like to add a unique twist to our spirits. Backwards ages each of its whiskeys individually in 53-gallon barrels, leaving the barrel only when the whiskey has fully matured.

Process & Products Notes: **Backwards Contortionist Gin** is a contemporary-style gin with fresh citrus as its heart, utilizing fourteen botanicals to produce a bright citrus-forward gin that's perfect for a cocktail. **Sword Swallower Rum** is made with a special Brazilian organic evaporated cane juice. Fermented with a tequila strain of yeast, the rum carries a unique blend of tropical fruit notes and grassy herbaceous flavors.

An old-world Russian-style vodka, **Ringleader Vodka** retains a soft, sweet flavor inherent to wheat vodka. Bourbon yeast is used to produce a smooth creamy palate.

Featured Product

Strongman Navy Strength Gin emerged from an experiment. "It was inspired," Pollock explains, "by a gin cocktail we had in

ADDRESS	CONTACT INFORMATION
158 Progress Circle	307-472-1275
Mills, WY 82644	backwardsdistilling.com
	facebook.com/backwardsdistilling
OWNER(S)	
Chad Pollock, Amber Pollock,	TASTING ROOM: Yes
Bill Pollock, Kathy Pollock	TOURS: Yes

London that paired a piney dry gin with black pepper-corn." The Backwards team set out to create a gin with that intriguing combination. Distillation began in November 2017.

Starting with their base vodka, which is distilled from locally-grown corn and beet sugar, they made numerous trial batches to obtain the maximum juniper flavor in the spirit. Then they added flavoring botanicals, with cubeb berry as the signature component. Typically used in gin as a background note, cubeb berry has a primary role in Strongman, adding notes of peppercorn spice with a citrus undertone. "We backed that up," Pollack explains "with grains of paradise adding an earthy, citrus, and spicy flavor to the middle of the gin. We tie it all together finally with the element that inspired the project: black peppercorn, green peppercorn, and pink pepper-corn."

Mi Cassis Es Su Cassis

- 1-1/2 oz STRONGMAN GIN
- 1-1/2 oz pineapple juice
- 3/4 oz cassis liqueur
- 1/2 oz fresh lime juice

Shake all ingredients with ice, strain over crushed ice, grate cinnamon on top and garnish with a cinnamon stick for aroma. Pineapple complements the peppercorn profile and black currant liqueur adds depth, making a perfect match with the resinous pine flavor from the juniper and cubeb berries in Strongman Gin.

Distiller's Tasting Notes: Chad's profile of Strongman Gin: A big, bold 114 proof gin focused on juniper and peppercorn flavors. On the palate, this gin starts with a rich resinous pine and a sap-like, slightly sweet, interpretation of the juniper. This is followed by a wave of peppercorn that brings a pleasant warmth and prickly spice to the middle of the gin. Finally, as the spice subsides, a floral and fruity flavor from the pink peppercorn dominates the finish.

Jackson Hole Still Works

JACKSON HOLE Still Works began distilling in 2015. Their spirits now include bourbon, malt and rye whiskeys, gin and vodka, and are widely distributed in Wyoming and Idaho.

Philosophy: Two long-time friends—Chas Marsh and Travis Goodman—created the company to be community focused, a leader in sustainable production, and one that would embody the quality of the natural environment, where they have spent many years together on the rivers and in the mountains of Wyoming.

Process & Products Notes: At Jackson Hole Still Works, every ounce of spirit is handmade at the distillery using only grains farmed in Wyoming.

Their **Highwater Vodka** exemplifies this standard, using Wyoming-farmed non-GMO corn and oats to craft a naturally gluten-free, crisp and velvety spirit. Highwater is distilled to the style of old-world, hand-crafted vodkas to maintain the integrity of its high-quality raw materials.

Goodman describes their vodka: "The nose provides hints of sweetness reminiscent of a fine custard, and the palate yields notes of Asian pear with an incredibly smooth finish, leaving a velvety mouthfeel. Enjoy it as it is, simply poured over ice with a twist, or blended into your favorite cocktail. Sure to inspire dreams of the wide open spaces, mountain peaks and river valleys that make us love the American Mountain West from where this spirit is born."

ADDRESS
3940 S Eagle View Drive
Jackson, WY 83001

OWNER(S)
Chas Marsh, Travis Goodman

CONTACT INFORMATION
307-699-8998
jhstillworks.com
facebook.com/jhstillworks

TASTING ROOM: Yes, call ahead
TOURS: Yes

Featured Product

Great Grey Gin is a handcrafted, ultra small-batch spirit, distilled from entirely non-GMO corn and oats harvested from the Big Horn Basin of Wyoming. The water is some of the purest in the world, naturally granite-filtered through the crags of the Teton Mountain Range and the headwaters of the Snake River.

A combination of botanical steeping and vapor infusion is employed in the distillation process to yield the most delicate and smooth character in this classic spirit.

Distiller's Tasting Notes:
Our botanical blend provides a slight twist to the typical London Dry style, yielding perfectly balanced hints of citrus,

---

The Hef

- 2 oz Great Grey Gin
- 1/2 oz Dolin Dry Vermouth
- 3/4 oz St. Germain
- 1/2 lemon squeezed (about 1/2 oz lemon juice)
- Dash of bitters

Shaken, strained and served up with lemon twist garnish for a bright and tantalizing cocktail.

---

spice and fresh floral notes in conjunction with the traditional juniper and coriander essences. Great Grey is rich enough to enjoy up, just with a twist, and will grace a classic Gin & Tonic or any of your favorite gin cocktails.

WYOMING WHISKEY

WYOMING WHISKEY, a family-owned distillery, makes bourbon, rye and specialty whiskeys. Their products are distributed in at least thirty-four states, including Colorado, New Mexico and Wyoming.

Philosophy: Wyoming Whiskey has a motto: Wyoming. Family. Whiskey—In That Order. They hold that the quality of their products is an expression of the Wyoming land and 100-percent local ingredients, describing this ethos with another saying: "Our company and products are a collaboration between our partners and 97,818 square miles of Wyoming. The state defines us."

Process & Product Notes: **Outryder Straight American Whiskey** is crafted from two distinct mash bills. One is 48% winter rye, 40% corn and 12% malted barley, and the second reflects a traditional bourbon mash bill. Outryder Whiskey therefore stands apart—neither a bourbon and nor a true rye. Bottled in bond at 100 proof, the result is a singular spirit for sipping or making cocktails.

Wyoming Whiskey Double Cask is a fully-matured five-year-old bourbon finished in Pedro Ximenez sherry casks. A smooth, full-bodied bourbon, with a distinctly sweeter finish. Available in select markets in limited supply.

Their **Single Barrel Bourbon** is one barrel selected for its noteworthy character and taste to receive the special label of Single Barrel. Roughly one out of every 100 barrels exhibits such special characteristics. This product is only available each November and in very limited quantities.

ADDRESS
100 S. Nelson Street
Kirby, Wyoming 82430

OWNER(S)
Brad Mead, Kate Mead, David DeFazio

CONTACT INFORMATION
307-864-2116
wyomingwhiskey.com
facebook.com/WyomingWhiskey

TASTING ROOM: Yes
TOURS: Yes

Featured Product

Small Batch Bourbon Whiskey has a traditional bourbon recipe, while its locale and non-GMO local ingredients—that is, its terroir—bring distinctive characteristics. All water used to produce the bourbon has been stored for some 6,000 years in a limestone aquifer lying a mile beneath Manderson, Wyoming. Fermentation and distillation occur on-site in four 2,500-gallon fermentation tanks and a traditional continuous distillation system, with a 38-foot tall Vendome copper column still and doubler.

Aged at 115 proof in new, 53-gallon, charred American white oak barrels, the whiskey rests in unconditioned warehouses. This allows it to experience large seasonal temperature fluctuations and, more importantly, extreme diurnal temperature swings—in summer even exceeding a 130-degree difference. The whiskey therefore ages more quickly and effectively.

RASPBERRY SMASH

- 2 oz Wyoming Whiskey Small Batch Bourbon
- 3/4 oz fresh lemon juice
- 3/4 oz raspberry syrup
- 1 mint leaf

Mix lemon juice and raspberr syrup, then swirl into the Small Batch Bourbon. Garnish with mint.

Distiller's Tasting Notes: The Small Batch Bourbon has a dark amber color and floral aroma, with hints of vanilla bean and caramel pudding. The palate is floral with brown baking spices and browned butter, vanilla crème, caramel and a touch of cinnamon. Mouthfeel is light and smooth, with a hint of mint; vanilla bean and cinnamon spice fill the mouth cavity. The finish is medium length with toffee, spice and vanilla fade.

ADDITIONAL COMPANIES

COLORADO

● 12 POINT DISTILLERY

802 S. Public Road
Lafayette, Colorado 80026
303-310-7223
12pointdistillery.com

This family-owned, woman-owned distillery produces small-batch vodka and liqueurs. Rum and gin are coming soon.

● 39 NORTH SPIRITS

Eagle, Colorado
970-376-2632
39northspirits.com

This team has three products: a 10-year straight bourbon, 8-year straight rye whiskey and a spiced whiskey. To retain the maximum flavor profile, they do not chill filter their spirits.

● 808 DISTILLERY

PO Box 2187
Edwards, Colorado 81632
970-390-0191
808distill.com

Since 2014, they have made Leo's Limoncello, a lemon liqueur. More recent additions to their lineup include Red Canyon Rum and Red Canyon Spiced Rum, June Creek Gin and Vail Valley Vodka.

● ALTITUDE SPIRITS

2805 Wilderness Place
Boulder Colorado 80301
720-249-2463
altitudespirits.com

Altitude Spirits offers a portfolio of organic craft spirits from around the world. They have produced their organic flagship product, Vodka 14, since 2005. In 2011, they became the exclusive American importer for Papagayo Spiced and Platinum Rums, Juniper Green Gin, and Highland Harvest Scotch Whisky, all of which are organically produced.

● ARCHETYPE DISTILLERY

119 S. Broadway
Denver, Colorado 80209
303-999-0105
archetypedistillery.com

The owners have renovated a historic theater in Denver and are using innovative processes and ingredients for their gin and vodka.

● ART OF THE SPIRITS

P.O. Box 19914
Denver, Colorado 80219
720-530-9732
artofthespirits.com

Art of the Spirits produces bourbon and rye whiskeys. A distinction of the company is their work with nationally-known artists who create labels adorned with attractive women from the late 17th and early 18th centuries. These images are offered in various sizes and, with the bottles, make for collectors' items.

● BIG FAT PASTOR

6754 N. Franklin Avenue
Loveland, Colorado 80538
970-619-8127
bigfatpastorspirits.com

Big Fat Pastor Spirits is a family-owned micro distillery. Using Rocky Mountain water and local grains and botanicals, they are making small-batch gin and vodka for their local community to enjoy.

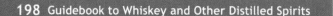

● CO-NE ● CO-Metro ● CO-SE ● CO-NW ● CO-SW

● BLANK AND BOOTH

999 Vallejo Street
Denver, Colorado 80204
406-861-7501
blankandbooth.com

Blank and Booth open ferments products in 500-gallon cypress fermenters so that their spirits gather wild yeast, making every batch unique. Their products include corn whiskey, with a variety of infusion treatments, and vodka.

● BOATHOUSE DISTILLERY

7728 County Road 150
Salida, Colorado 81201
719-221-3307
boathousedistillery.com

Boathouse Distillery finishes and bottles a bourbon that is sourced from southern-state distillers. They also offer a white dog whiskey, vodka, rum and a blue agave tequila imported from Mexico.

● BOUCK BROTHERS

2731 Colorado Boulevard
Idaho Springs, Colorado 80452
303-567-2547
bouckbros.com

Bouck Brothers Distillery is a grain-to-glass, small-batch distillery and tasting room. They use Colorado grain and wild Colorado yeast to make a bourbon and other products including a coffee whiskey.

● COCKPIT CRAFT DISTILLERY

4893 Galley Road
Colorado Springs, Colorado 80915
720-299-0071
cockpitdistillery.com

Cockpit features several whiskeys, including bourbon. They also have an apple pie white dog and a couple of rums. All these expressions are fashioned into cocktails in their tasting room which is heavy in aircraft decor.

● COYOTE GOLD

6419 Falcon Ridge Court
Fort Collins, Colorado 80525
970-227-1455
coyotegold.info

Coyote Gold is a bottled margarita product made with a premium tequila imported from Mexico. They blend in their own handcrafted orange liqueur, pure fruit juice, pure cane sugar and all-natural citrus flavors.

● DENVER DISTILLERY

244 S. Broadway
Denver, Colorado 80209
720-381-3226
denverdistillery.com

Denver Distillery serves cocktails using house spirits served with savory & sweet pastries in a cozy environment.

● DEVIATION DISTILLING

900 W. First Avenue, #150
Denver, Colorado 80223
720-683-0588
deviationdistilling.com

Deviation Distilling produces gin with the philosophy to challenge the traditional manufacturing of spirits by borrowing from tradition, leveraging Colorado grown grain and applying unique techniques based on their custom-built equipment.

● ELWOOD DISTILLING CO.

5757 Arapahoe Avenue, Unit A2
Boulder, Colorado 80303
720-771-5186
elwooddistillingco.com

The folks at Elwood make a single-malt whiskey with four kinds of malted barley. They use open-air fermenters and slowly distill the whiskey two times in their hand-hammered copper pot still. The whiskey is matured in charred American oak barrels and finished with toasted cherry wood staves.

● HALE & BRADFORD

335 Mountain Avenue
Berthoud, Colorado 80513
303-884-1287
haleandbradford.com

Hale & Bradford are bottlers of bourbon, vodka and rum.

● HOGBACK DISTILLERY

4840 Van Gordon Street #600
Wheat Ridge, Colorado 80033
720-357-9320
hogbackdistillery.com

Hogback Distillery offerings include a whiskey produced using Scottish techniques, with 100% malted barley processed through a pair of copper pot stills and matured in used white oak casks. They also have a high-corn bourbon, a high-rye bourbon and a high-rye whiskey.

● IRONTON DISTILLERY

3636 Chestnut Place
Denver, Colorado 80216
Phone: n/a
irontondistillery.com

Inspired by the adventurous spirit of Colorado, Ironton Distillery hand crafts a variety of products, including small-batch, farm-to-flask specialties and creative house-made cocktails.

● J & L DISTILLING

4843 Pearl Street
Boulder, Colorado 80304
720-400-1907
jldistilling.com

J & L uses Louisiana sugar cane to make their three primary products: SNO Vodka, SNO Gin and their SNO Liqueur. The gin uses a vapor infusing process to extract essential oils from selected botanicals.

● LEE SPIRITS

110 E Boulder Street
Colorado Springs, Colorado 80903
719-205-4392
leespirits.com

A dry gin is the flagship product offered by Lee Spirits. They also produce lavender, strawberry and pepper-spiced gins. Their five liqueurs have fruit, crème de violette, crème de cacao, crème de rose and herbal recipes.

● MTN DISTILLERS

P.O. Box 1768
Eagle, Colorado 81631
970-376-0695

Each batch of their gin is handcrafted using only Colorado botanicals blended with fresh citrus zest and finished with mountain spring water. MTN GIN takes a subtle approach to the juniper component, focusing on the floral and citrus elements.

● MYTHOLOGY DISTILLERY

3622 Tejon Street
Denver, Colorado 80211
Phone: n/a
mythologydistillery.com

Opening announced for summer of 2018.

● PEAK SPIRITS

26567 North Road
Hotchkiss, Colorado 81419
970-361-4249
peakspirits.com

CapRock gin, vodka and brandies are made at the Peak Spirits Distillery at Jack Rabbit Hill Farm. All products are USDA-certified organic, and some are Demeter-certified biodynamic. They process first-use irrigation water, living soils and small blocks of craft-farmed fruit in a little copper still.

● SANGRE DISTILLERIES

25 Ranchview Loop
Westcliffe, Colorado 81252
719-783-0296

High in the Wet Mountain Valley, Sangre Distilleries crafts small-batch spirits using Rocky Mountain water and all natural ingredients. They distill, bottle and label all by hand, while adding no artificial flavors or colors to their rums, white dog or single malt whiskey.

● SKI BUM RUM DISTILLERY

[New location announcement in 2018.]
970-401-2271
skibumrum.com

Ski Bum Rum distillery is known for making spiced rum and coconut rum. They offer distinctive flavors using superior spices and ingredients like real vanilla bean and wildflower honey.

● SNITCHING LADY

526 Front Street
Fairplay, Colorado 80440
484-747-5454
snitchingladydistillery.com

A micro distillery specializing in small-batch rye whiskey and grappa.

● SPIRITS OF THE ROCKIES

2907 Graneron Lane, Unit A
Pueblo, Colorado 81005
719-661-1879
www.spiritsoftherockies.com

Spirits of the Rockies makes a grain neutral spirit, white dog and rye whiskeys, and an agavé product. Their white dog was inspired by traditional family stories and recipes from the 1900s. The old moonshine jug handed down for generations inspired the jug their spirits are bottled in today.

● STORM KING

41 W. Main Street
Montrose, Colorado 81401
970-209-8663
stormkingdistilling.com

Storm King Distilling makes gin with local juniper from the Colorado Uncompahgre Plateau and agavé spirits using yeast and organic Blue agavé nectar from Mexico. Their goal is to produce quality spirits at affordable prices for all spirit consumers.

● SUERTE TEQUILA

1930 14th Street

Boulder 80302
720-310-5825
drinksuerte.com

The tequilas from Suerte are distilled, matured and bottled in Mexico. They have three types: blanco, rested two months in stainless steel; reposado, matured seven months in charred American oak barrels; and añejo, matured for twenty-four months. Their extra añejo is double distilled and matured for seven years.

● THE BLOCK

900 Larimer Street
Denver, Colorado 80205
303-484-9033
theblockdistillingco.com

The Block Distilling Co. blends culinary and chemistry methods to artfully create two gins and a vodka.

● THE FAMILY JONES

3245 Osage Street
Denver, Colorado 80211
303-481-8185
thefamilyjones.co

They are known as a destination for tasty food and spirits.

● TIGHE BROTHERS DISTILLERY

4200 Milwaukee St
Denver, Colorado 80207
303-635-6177
tighedistillery.com

Their primary product is bourbon distilled with the owner's custom recipe using Colorado grain for specific flavors and processed precisely for richness.

● VAPOR DISTILLERY

5311 Western Avenue #180
Boulder, Colorado 80301
303-997-6134
vapordistillery.com

The flagship spirit from Vapor is a new western-style gin, with less juniper and combined with lavender, hibiscus, citrus peel, green tea and other botanicals. Their bourbon mash bill is of 51% corn, 44% malted barley and 5% rye.

● WEAVER'S SPIRITS

6360 Arapahoe Court
Parker, Colorado 80134
720-431-7432
www.weaversspirits.com

Weaver's Spirits products are bottled in Colorado, and each expression of Weaver's celebrates a different Colorado 14er, identified by the die-cut mountain image on their labels. Their first offering is a light whiskey and it celebrates Mount Massive, the second highest peak in the Rocky Mountains.

● WESTERN GAEL

5405 W. 56th Avenue, Unit C
Arvada, Colorado 80002
303-431-4949
westerngael.com

Scheduled to open in summer 2018, their dream is to lead the American restoration of single pot-still whiskey by making perhaps the only such spirit in North America using traditional triple distillation. This process will honor Gaelic-Irish tradition.

NEW MEXICO

AZTEC SPIRITS

36 Bisbee Court
Santa Fe, New Mexico 87508
575-751-7168
aztecspirits.com

Aztec has two brands: Aztec and Dire Wolf, and both feature bourbon and vodka expressions. The bourbons are filtered four times and aged in oak barrels with oak chips. Their vodkas are distilled five times and filtered four times including chill-filtered and charcoal-filtered.

BROKEN TRAIL SPIRITS+BREW

2921 Stanford Drive NE
Albuquerque, New Mexico 87107
505-221-6281
brokentrailspirits.com

Broken Trail distills their Holy Ghost Vodka with 100-percent corn and Bull-of-the-Woods Gin with local botanicals, including prickly pear, neomexicanus hops and juniper. Tres Pistolas Bourbon Whiskey employs locally grown corn and a small percentage of smoked barley, adding a little smokiness to balance the sweetness from the corn.

DON QUIXOTE DISTILLERY

18057-A NM 84/285
Santa Fe, New Mexico 87506
505-695-0817
dqdistillery.com

For their bourbon, Don Quixote uses organic New Mexico blue corn. They malt their grain to convert the starch to sugar. At higher elevation, they separate the alcohol at a lower temperature for a softer whiskey. They have two bourbons and a rye whiskey that follow this process, and also produce a gin, vodka and brandy that take advantage of local ingredients.

GLENCOE DISTILLERY

27489 US Highway 70
Glencoe, New Mexico 88324
575-430-2325
facebook.com/GlencoeDistillery

Their products--which they describe as "The Spirits of the West embodied in the Mountains by smoke, outlaws, horses and grit"--include rum, vodka, gin, coffee liqueur and whiskey. They source ingredients from their locale in the southern Rocky Mountains and high desert of New Mexico, which is rich in grains, fruit and nut orchards and botanicals.

HOLLOW SPIRITS

1324 1st Street, NW
Albuquerque, New Mexico 87102
505-433-2766
hollowspirits.com

Hollow Spirits is a craft distillery opening in 2018 near downtown Albuquerque. They plan to serve all things craft and local, with their own spirits as the base of a seasonal craft cocktail menu.

KGB SPIRITS

183 County Road 41
Alcalde, New Mexico 87511
505-404-6101
kgbspirits.com

Taos Lightning is reportedly the oldest spirit brand in America, originally distilled in 1820. Made from 95-percent rye, it's aged in new charred American oak barrels. They have two other ryes, plus their Los Luceros Hacienda Gin and the potato-based Vodka Viracocha.

LITTLE TOAD CREEK DISTILLERY

200 N. Bullard
Silver City, New Mexico 88061
575-956-6144
littletoadcreek.com

Little Toad Creek produces small-batch vodka, rum, whiskey and liqueurs with a hand-built copper still. The distiller's favorite is their aged whiskey, Sapo Grande.

STILL SPIRITS

120 NW Marble Avenue
Albuquerque, New Mexico 87102
501-750-3138
facebook.com/stillspiritsabq

Still Spirits is a new distillery producing vodka and gin. Their tasting room, while small, has a fun feel.

WYOMING

CHRONICLES DISTILLING

1506 Thomas Avenue
Cheyenne, Wyoming 82001
307-214-1854
facebook.com/ChroniclesDistilling

Chronicles Distilling, newly established in downtown Cheyenne, is a veteran-owned family distillery making spirits with locally-sourced grains.

COWBOY COUNTRY DISTILLING

1 Cobblestone Drive
Pinedale, Wyoming 82941
307-367-2331

Cowboy Country just opened their 10,000 square-foot distillery in Pinedale, where they are producing gin and vodka, their latest being a jalapeño bacon vodka.

GEYSER DISTILLING

1326 Beck Avenue
Cody, Wyoming 82414
307-899-3815
geyserdistilling.com

Geyser Distilling makes their whiskey with local corn and their vodka from grapes from their own Buffalo Jump Winery, co-located with the distillery. Other products include a vodka from sugar beets, a bourbon, and an Irish-style single-malt whiskey. [Open seasonally.]

KOLTISKA DISTILLERY

644 Crook Street
Sheridan, Wyoming 82801
307-673-7307
koltiska.com

The Koltiska family, homesteaders in Sheridan since the late 1800s, continue to produce grains but now also make a vodka and three liqueurs. Koltiska Original is a 60 proof, light spiced cinnamon liqueur, and their K90 is the Original but bottled at 90 proof. The Wintermint is a 60-proof spearmint and peppermint liqueur.

PINE BLUFFS DISTILLING

322 N. Beach Street
Pine Bluffs, Wyoming 82082
503-249-0968
pinebluffsdistilling.com

With a philosophy of minimal waste, Pine Bluffs makes their vodkas ethically and responsibly. Spent grains are returned to the farm to feed local livestock. They have their own onsite malt house.

GLOSSARY

TERM	DEFINITION
ABV	Alcohol by volume is the percentage of alcohol in a given volume of liquid. In the United States, both ABV and Proof, which is simply ABV doubled, are shown on the product label: 40% ABV equals 80 proof.
Age	Age is the period after distillation and before bottling that distilled spirits have been stored in barrels or wood containers.
Angel's share	The portion of a spirit in an aging barrel that's lost to evaporation.
Backset	The thin, watery part of a previously distilled batch of whiskey mash that is added – or "set back" – into the next batch. Also known as sour mash, setback, stillage or spent beer.
Barrel	Round, convex, watertight, wooden container made by wrapping heated, bent oak staves around flat oak end panels and binding them in a circle with metal hoops. While an American new oak whiskey barrel has a capacity of 53 gallons, associated barrel capacities are: kegs that contain up to 25 gallons and casks, butts, hogsheads and puncheons that have capacities that range from 60 to 340 gallons. Small craft distillers are using barrel sizes of 30, 15, 5 and even 2 gallons to accelerate the aging process
Barrel proof	Whiskey bottled at the proof it comes from the barrel. No water is added before bottling, so these spirits are higher proof than others. Commonly referred to as barrel strength.
Beer still	A giant apparatus in which the main component is a very tall metal column used to separate the alcohol from the water in the distiller's beer by vaporizing the alcohol content. The spirit produced is called low wines.
Brandy	A distilled wine aged in a barrel.
Charring	The process that sets fire to the interior of barrels and creates a layer of charred wood. Distillers can choose from four levels of char, with #1 Char being the lightest burn and a #4 Char the heaviest burn. End plates are generally "toasted."
Column still	Also known as a continuous or coffee still, it is a tall cylinder with sections divided by plates where wash falls down while steam rises upward, separating the alcohol for the wash. Unlike a pot still where wash is run in batches, a column still runs continuously for a higher volume of product in less time.
Cordials or liqueurs	Products obtained by mixing or redistilling distilled spirits with (or over) fruits, flowers, plants, or their pure juices, or other natural flavoring materials; or with extracts derived from infusions, percolation, or maceration of such materials. The finished product must contain sugar, dextrose, or levulose, or a combination thereof, in an amount that is not less than two and one-half percent (2.5%) of its weight.

TERM	DEFINITION
Craft spirits	The products of an independently-owned distillery with maximum annual sales of 52,000 cases where the product is physically distilled and bottled on-site. **Requirements** *Independently-Owned:* Less than 25% of the craft distillery (distilled spirits plant or DSP) is owned or controlled (or equivalent economic interest) by alcoholic beverage industry members who are not themselves craft distillers. *Small-Scale:* Maximum annual sales are less than 100,000 proof gallons. *Distilled by the DSP*: The spirit must have been run through a still by a certified craft producer, and the TTB-approved label must state "Distilled By" followed by the name of the DSP. *Hands-on Production*: Craft distillers produce spirits that reflect the vision of their principal distillers using any combination of traditional or innovative techniques including fermenting, distilling, re-distilling, blending, infusing or warehousing.
Cuts	Stages in pot still distillation where the stream of alcohol is divided into heads (or foreshots), hearts, and tails (feints). The cuts are made to get the maximum amount of clean spirit. Heads and tails, which contain impurities, often are redistilled.
Distiller's beer	A thick, fermented mash of cooked grains, water and yeast that is transferred from the fermenter to the beer still for the first distillation. Often referred to as wash.
Distilled spirits plant (DSP)	An establishment which is qualified under CFR Title 27 to conduct distilled spirits operations.
Fermentation	The process by which yeast transforms sugar into alcohol and carbon dioxide.
Fermenter	A giant tub made of metal or cypress in which the mash of cooked grains and water meets the yeast. They mingle, the yeast begins to act on sugars in the grain, and fermentation occurs over a few days. This produces alcohol within the mash and turns it into wash, also called distiller's beer.
High wines	The final spirit produced by the secondary distillation, ready for aging.
Light Whiskey	Whiskey produced in the U.S. at more than 80% alcohol by volume (160 proof) [but less than 95% alcohol by volume (190 proof)] and stored in used or uncharred new oak containers.
Low wines	The name of the spirit after it has passed through the beer or continuous still for its first distillation.
Malting	Wetting any grain to start partial germination and then heating or roasting to stop the germination. Barley, the most commonly malted grain, contains enzymes that convert starches into the fermentable sugars on which yeast feeds. These enzymes are not present in unmalted grains.

TERM	DEFINITION
Mash Tun	Large vessel that contains the mixture of cooked grains and water (mash) before the yeast is added to start fermentation.
Mash bill	The grain recipe used to make whiskey. An example would be 55% corn, 30% wheat and 15% barley.
Natural Spirits	Distilled spirits produced from any material at or above 190 proof. If they are bottled, they are bottled at not less than 80 proof.
Nose	The aroma of a whiskey or other spirit.
Pot still	A still characterized by a round, normally copper base where wash is heated and alcohol separates and rises up through a neck and then through a lyne arm and eventually down for collection.
Proof	The ethyl alcohol content of a liquid at 60° F, stated as twice the percent of ethyl alcohol by volume (ABV).
Rectifier	Someone who purchases raw alcohol and makes a palatable whiskey by filtering it and adding flavoring compounds or, in relation to the equipment for distilling, it is a final column still used to produce or rectify a new spirit.
Sambuca	An Italian aniseed-flavored liqueur.
Single-barrel whiskey	Whiskey drawn from one barrel that has not been mingled with any other whiskeys.
Spirit still	One of the types of stills used to accomplish the second distillation of American whiskey.
Straight whiskey	Whiskey that has been matured for at least two years.
Stripping still	A single-column still used for first distillation in making whiskey.
Tennessee whiskey	A whiskey made in Tennessee that has gone through the Lincoln County process. This means their white dog is filtered through 10 feet of hardwood charcoal and a white wool blanket.
TTB	The Alcohol and Tobacco Tax and Trade Bureau of the Department of the Treasury is the regulatory organization for the distillation industry.
Warehouse	The general term for the building used for barrel maturation. In the U.S. they are sometimes referred to as rackhouses or rickhouses because of the wooden rails or "ricks" used to hold the barrels.
Wort	The product of brewing before fermentation which results in a type of distiller's beer. It is ready to ferment and become wash.
Yeast	A living organism that feeds on fermentable sugars, transforming them to beverage alcohol, congeners, carbon dioxide, and heat.

INDEX

NOTES